Human resource management in the public sector

Peter Smart

Katsuhiro Inazawa

Kwansei Gakuin University Press

Human resource management in the public sector

Peter Smart and Katsuhiro Inazawa

©2011 by Peter Smart, Katsuhiro Inazawa

Kwansei Gakuin University Press
1-1-155 Uegahara, Nishinomiya, Hyogo Prefecture, JAPAN
ISBN: 978-4-86283-091-3

Human resource management
in the public sector

Contents

List of figures

List of tables

About the authors

Preface

PART 1   CHALLENGES AND MODELS OF HRM

Introduction to Part 1

    1   A challenging subject for challenging times

    2   Models and maps of HRM

PART 2   ASPECTS OF HRM

Introduction to Part 2

    3   Strategic insights and solutions

    4   Organisation design and development

    5   Resourcing and talent planning

    6   Learning and talent development

    7   Performance and reward

    8   Employee relations and engagement

PART 3 DELIVERY MODELS AND NEXT GENERATION HRM

Introduction to Part 3

    9   Leading and managing the human resources function

   10   HR in the public sector: the next steps?

Subject index

Author index

This work was supported in part by a Grant-in-aid for Scientific Research (No. 19203022) from the Japanese Ministry of Education, Culture, Sports, Science and Technology.

List of figures

Figure		Page
1.1	The seven challenges for HRM in the public sector	17
1.2	Seven aspects of 'the public sector'	21
2.1	The HRM map simplified	36
2.2	Buyens and de Vos Value-added Model of HRM: Involvement of HRM in decision-making processes	40
2.3	Buyens and de Vos Value-added Model of HRM: The added value of HRM at different moments of influence in the decision-making process	41
2.4	Buyens and de Vos Value-added Model of HRM: An integrated model for the added value of HRM	42
2.5	The HR Professional Map	45
3.1	Process model for business planning	64
3.2	Information used in workforce planning	65
3.3	Workforce planning roles and responsibilities	66
3.4	Challenges and enablers of workforce planning	67
4.1	Illustration of types of formal organisational relationships	75
4.2	Example of service-based matrix organisation structure	76
4.3	Atkinson's Model of the Flexible Firm	78
4.4	Representation of Handy's shamrock organisation	79

4.5	The model of perpetual transition management	82
4.6	The intervention strategy model of change	83
5.1	Enhancing talent management in the public sector	97
5.2	Outline redeployment and redundancy procedure	102
7.1	The interlocking dimensions of performance	122
10.1	Assessment tool based on Buyens and de Vos (1999)	161
10.2	Assessment tool based on CIPD HR Profession map (2010)	161

List of tables

Table		Page
2.1	The changing roles of HRM	34
2.2	Guest's model of HRM	39
4.1	Key questions of organisation design	72

Apart from any fair dealing for the purposes of research or private study, or criticism or review, as permitted under relevant copyright legislation, this publication may only be reproduced, stored or transmitted, in any form or by any means, with the prior permission in writing by the publishers. Enquiries concerning publication outside these terms shall be sent to the publishers:

The rights of Peter Smart and Katsuhiro Inazawa to be identified as the authors of this work have been asserted by them in accordance with the relevant international copyright legislation.

Kwansei Gakuin University Press and the authors have made every effort to trace and acknowledge copyright holders. If any source has been overlooked, Kwansei Gakuin University Press would be pleased to redress this for future editions.

About the authors

Dr Peter Smart was employed in the human resource management function in the UK public sector for 30 years and then later as Professor of Human Resource Management at a UK business school. His teaching and research interests include the impact of HR on the management and strategic success of the public sector. He is a Visiting Professor to Kwansei Gakuin University.

Dr Katsuhiro Inazawa was employed in the budget and finance division in the Japanese public sector for 15 years and from 2006/07 as a Professor of Institute of Business and Accounting (IBA) of Kwansei Gakuin University.

Preface

**The challenge of the global recession:
a key influence on this book**

I was asked to prepare this book just as the global recession was at its depth. It was clear that the public sector in many countries was going to become a victim of budget cuts and other fiscal measures that would impact adversely on public sector employment. This, in turn, would pose potentially new challenges for politicians, senior management and those engaged in the human resource management (HR) function. Just as we completed the final draft, in late October 2010, the true impact of the financial constraints on the public sector was becoming much clearer, in Europe, the USA and elsewhere in the world.

In the UK, the coalition government announced the results of its comprehensive spending review on 27 October 2010. This involved the most severe cuts in the budgets of many public services since 1945. Only the National Health Service in England and the international development budget said to be immune from budget reductions: not even the defence and police budgets remained unscathed. In parallel with the cuts, a two year public sector pay freeze was imposed on many public servants, and the public service pension scheme was amended, to require employees to make increased contributions in return for less generous benefits.

Elsewhere in Europe, governments in countries as diverse as Greece, Spain, France and Ireland implemented unprecedented budget cuts. In some of these countries, there were strikes and at times quite violent demonstrations against government policy. In the USA, many state and city governments were tantamount to bankrupt and close to defaulting on the payment of staff wages. There, too, many public authorities imposed pay freezes and other restrictions on staff costs, such as the non-filling of vacancies and encouraging staff to consider reductions in working time, sabbaticals and early retirement.

The impact of the global financial crisis was inevitably a major influence on the writing of the book, since many politicians, managers and HR practitioners were entering territory of which they had little or no previous experience. What is more, the impact of the recession is likely to be felt in the public sector for some years to come. There are many signs that the structure and size of the public sector is in transition. For example, it has been forecast that in the UK more than 500,000 public sector jobs will be lost by 2015. New models of service delivery are being trialled in many countries, including the USA, the UK and Sweden. Some involve new forms of outsourcing and contracting to external agencies, including the third sector (also called the voluntary or not-for-profit sector). Others rely on the development of shared services, whereby two or more public agencies will use a single delivery service.

**The challenge of the global recession:
new structures and ways of working**
These developments will require new organisational structures and new management relationships. They might involve the development of new pay structures and conditions of employment. Fewer employees may be required to provide the same or greater levels of output, using new information and communications technologies (ICT) or streamlined processes based on the precepts of total quality management (TQM) and *kaizen*. The emphasis is likely to be increasingly on the recruitment and development of high performing talent, expected to achieve clearly stated objectives that relate directly to the strategic aims of the organisation.

It is argued throughout this book that there is a key role for HR practitioners in the public sector, in helping their employing agencies to develop and implement staffing strategies that reflect overall organisational objectives during the continuing period of financial restraint.

The challenge of the global recession: not the only influence on HR in the public sector

But the impact of the recession is not the only influence on the way in which the HR function is discharged. The book opens, in Essay 1, with an assessment of a number of challenges facing HR in the public sector, including political decision making, demography, technology, the environment and the increasing pace of change in organisations of every kind. It is proposed that it is incumbent on those engaged in HR in the public sector to ensure they have an enquiring mind. A critical understanding of these challenges and an ability to monitor the environment in which they are working, so that they are able proactively to recommend new approaches to HR as things round about them change.

The style and format of this book

In a book of this size, it is not feasible to provide a comprehensive guide to HR in the public sector. Indeed, it is not unusual for some of the standard textbooks about HR published in the UK and the USA to run to 800 or more pages, on larger paper size! Even textbooks about specific aspects of HR contain 300 or more pages, when they are designed for study at Masters' level.

Instead, it was decided to prepare a series of ten essays, each one of which will focus on a small number of key issues facing HR in the public sector in many different countries. Each of these essays is illustrated, either by reference to existing models and concepts, or by offering a range of links to other publications, journals and websites, from which readers may enhance their own knowledge and review case studies that might help them develop innovative approaches to HR in their own organisations.

This approach does mean that I have had to be selective in the materials that I present. I hope and trust that they will offer a fair reflection of the issues facing political leaders, managers and HR practitioners in the public sector, and will encourage readers to extend their studies to some of the other materials to which I refer.

Acknowledgement to Institute of Business and Accounting Kwansei Gakuin University

Finally, I wish to thank my good friend Professor Toshihiko Ishihara for asking me to prepare this book. It has offered me an intellectual and research challenge that has enhanced my own knowledge of HR in the public sector. There is so much that I have read myself that I have not been able to include in the present publication.

I hope that the trust that they have shown in my capacity to prepare the book has been rewarded with a publication that academics and practitioners will wish to read.

Dr Peter Smart
Aberdeen, Scotland

October 2010

Dedications

This book is dedicated to Margaret, my wife of 41 years, who has patiently got on with the business of life as I have sat for many hours in front of my computer.

Dr Peter Smart

Expression of gratitude

Our thanks are due to the many organisations, publishers and academics who have graciously granted me permission to reproduce items from other books, journals and websites.
In particular, special thanks are offered to
the UK Chartered Institute of Personnel and Development,
the US International Public Management Association
for Human Resources and the Boston Consulting Group
for permission to cite a range of professional materials,
and to authors Dirk Buyens and Ans de Vos, Linda Holbeche and Mee-Wan Cheung-Judge, and John Shields for personal permission to cite their academic work.

Introduction to Part 1

Part 1 consists of two essays.

Essay 1 provides a relatively detailed overview of the main current challenges facing the public sector in a number of countries across the world, and an assessment as to how these challenges impact on the HR function in the public sector. The aim is to stimulate proactive consideration as to how readers' own public sector organisations are responding, or might respond, to these different challenges.

Essay 2 then examines a number of accepted models of HR. These include one of the two most frequently cited models emanating from academic research undertaken in the USA in the early 1980s. The model emphasises the relationship of HR with interests both internal and external to the organisation, and the need for the development of HR outcomes that have benefits to the organisation, its employees and society at large.

Essay 2 also examines two models developed in Europe that seek to identify the continuum of roles that HR might play within the organisational structure, from administrative support to strategic leader. It also explains how cultural differences, for example, in East Asia, might affect the development of HR, compared with the more widely promoted models from the USA and Europe.

The aim of Essay 2 is to enable the reader to assess the range of ways in which HR might develop within organisations, particularly as a strategic partner to politicians and other senior managers as the organisation seeks to cope with the challenges assessed in Essay 1.

Essay 1
A CHALLENGING SUBJECT FOR CHALLENGING TIMES

Aims of essay 1
By the end of this essay, readers should be able to
- identify and explain the main challenges currently confronting human resource management in the public sector;
- assess the relative impact of each of these challenges on the public sector with which they are associated;
- conceptualise ways in which their part of the public sector might respond to the challenges.

HRM in the public sector:
A challenging subject for challenging times
The public sector is almost certainly under greater scrutiny, if not threat, on a global basis at the present time than it has been at any time since the Great Depression. After decades of developments in education, health care and social welfare, transport and infrastructure, and public protection and community development, governments across the world appear increasingly to be questioning the future role, structure and resourcing of the institutions they have created. New political approaches, the global economic crisis, changes in demography, the introduction of new technology and a range of other factors have all contributed to the challenge to the public sector as we have grown to know it.

One of the consequences will be a new order for those engaged in the human resource management (HR) function in public organisations. They will face a number of big tests, one of which will be to prove that they are more than an expensive bureaucratic on-cost; otherwise, some commentators suggest, the very survival of the HR function in the public sector will be threatened (see, for example, *People*

Management, 2010a). They will need to demonstrate that they understand the environment within which their part of the public sector is operating. They will need to demonstrate an ability to develop new HR strategies and plans that will ensure their employer adapts to the new circumstances with cost effective staffing structures. They will need to demonstrate that HR as a function adds value to the organisation (see, for example, *People Management*, 2010b, *People Management*, 2010c, www.ppma.org.uk, www.ipma-hr.org).

The purpose of this essay is to provide a broad overview of the changing environment in which the public sector is working. Without such an understanding it will be impossible to discern appropriate human resource strategies and to assist with their implementation.

From growth to retrenchment?

Of course, none of the individual challenges that the public sector is facing is new. Countries have been in recession before. Governments have regularly reorganised structures and service delivery. They have encouraged outsourcing and competitive tendering. Demographic changes do not happen overnight, but can be predicted years in advance using sophisticated forecasting models. It simply seems that the global economic crisis has become the catalyst for a root and branch review of what the public sector should do and how it should do it.

Since the late 1940s, there have been major developments in state and local government services such as education, health care, social welfare, the construction of new infrastructure, and the promotion by governments of international trade and international aid. Many new schools, universities and hospitals have been built. Innovative social support systems for the more disadvantaged members of society have been introduced. New highways, water and sewerage plant and power stations have been constructed. For several decades, most of these services in most countries were part of the public sector, and many still are. The public sector generally continued to absorb increasing proportions of GDP and to remain one of the largest employment sectors in the economy of most nations.

Since the 1980s, though, a number of trends have become increasingly apparent in countries as diverse as the USA, the UK, Sweden, Japan, Australia and New Zealand. The overall size of the public sector has been reduced by the deregulation, franchising and denationalisation of public transport, the privatisation of water and drainage, the introduction of toll roads built and operated by private companies and competition to nationalised mail services from privately owned companies such as TNT and DHL. The precepts of *Reinventing Government* (Osborne and Gaebler, 1992) and the New Public Management movement (see, for example, Barzelay, 2001), competitive tendering and outsourcing, the removal of publicly funded schools from local authority control under the *free school* (Swedish: *friskolor*) *movement* of Sweden and the *academy* programme in the UK, and similar developments have resulted in components of traditional public sector management being transferred to the control of other organisations.

Most recently, governments across the developed world have instituted programmes that threaten the continued existence of well-established services as a result of the economic crisis, leading to well-publicised strikes by public servants in France, Greece and Spain and threats of industrial action elsewhere. The point being made here is that HR professionals in the public sector have a key role to play, in helping their employing organisations to respond to these challenges in innovative ways that help ensure the continuation of service delivery on a cost effective basis (*People Management*, 2010b). The question may be asked, *how do we do this, when we don't know what the full effect of some of these challenges is?* One part of the answer is to prove that HR has the skills and abilities to manage in uncertain times, through innovation and creativity.

Fowler (1975:301), writing 35 years ago about HR in local government in the UK, commented that we can be certain that *the only predictable feature of the future is its unpredictability*. If that were true then, it is doubly true today. The remainder of this essay assesses the main challenges facing the public sector and offers some clues as to how HR can help respond to them.

The main challenges identified

Seven major challenges have been identified, as shown in Figure 1.1, each of which is applicable to some extent in every country in the world.

These challenges, individually and collectively, relate to the dynamic and, in many cases, rapidly changing environment within which the public sector is working. They reflect a series of uncertainties, including the direction of political decision making, the availability of tax

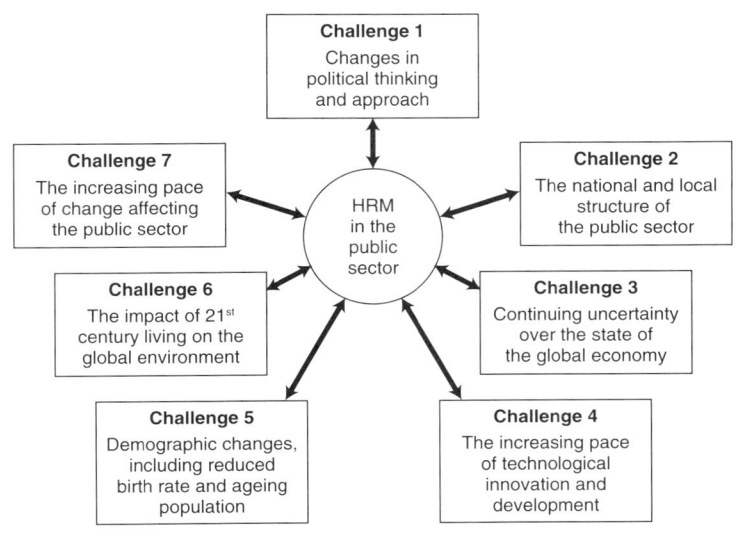

Figure 1.1
The seven challenges for HRM in the public sector
© Dr Peter Smart

revenues for public projects, the availability within the labour market of motivated employees (increasingly called *talent*) with the required knowledge and competencies to service the public sector, and the impact of new technology on working practices. Each of these challenges is assessed by way of setting the context within which the remainder of the book is written. The examples used are as up-to-date as publication has allowed, but since the context within which the public sector is working is itself constantly changing, it is incumbent on the reader to relate the models, concepts and approaches to HRM outlined in this book to the most current environment within which they are operating.

Challenge 1:
Changes in political thinking and approach
The public sector is under the control of, and subject to the decision-making of elected politicians and appointed boards, at national and local level. This is true whether the country is a long-established democracy, a developing democracy, a one-party state, a dictatorship or indeed under military control. It is generally accepted that it is the responsibility of national politicians to determine the general direction for their country and for regional and local politicians to develop and implement local policies within any constraints laid down by the supreme national decision-making body.

The balance of responsibility for the direct delivery of public services varies between countries, from the more highly centralised structures of the UK to the more acutely decentralised structures of Finland or Japan. In federal countries such as the USA and Germany, there is a more complex relationship between the various levels and types of government. Except in one party states and dictatorships, there is scope for disagreement between political representatives at different levels of government, especially where national government is of one political persuasion and local governments are of another.

Over the past two decades there has been evidence that politicians of all persuasions have been increasingly prepared to challenge their own traditions and thinking, with a view to delivering more cost efficient public services. Some of the innovations have already been referred to, including review of the structures of central and local government, outsourcing, competitive tendering, *best value* programmes and shared services.

Reviews of public sector efficiency have been commissioned (for example, the *Gershon Report*, 2004 in the UK). Specialist improvement organisations have been established (such as the Improvement Service for Scottish Local Government, www.improvementservice.org.uk). Academic departments (such as the Institute of Business and Accounting at the Kwansei Gakuin University, Japan, www.kwansei.ac.jp/english/graduate/g_iba.html, and the Kennedy School of Government at Harvard, www.khs.harvard.edu), private organisations (such as the Public Strategies Group, www.psgrp.com) and the major firms of management consultants all offer consultancy and advice on management and leadership in public bodies. New programmes aimed at further developing a more cohesive *joined up* public sector, on programmes such as the safeguarding of children (see also Total Place: a practitioner's guide to doing things differently (2010).

With the current pace of political decision-making, it is critical for those engaged in HR at the policy-making level in the public sector to be politically savvy and sensitive to the decisions and directions of the politicians they serve. It requires knowledge and the ability to keep a watching brief on the world around them (see Essay 2, the assessment of the Harvard Model of HRM, Beer *et al*, 1984) and, ideally, skills of forecasting how changes in political direction might impact on the public sector organisation they serve. At the most senior levels, it also requires the capacity to relate to and communicate with the political decision-makers, to discern and advise on how any changes in strategy or policy can best be implemented through the people who work for the organisation. In many countries, public servants are required to act apolitically. In this situation, they may well be required to implement strategies with which they may not personally be in political sympathy. To do otherwise could well jeopardise their continued employment.

Challenge 2:
The national and local structure of the public sector
The size, scope and structure of the public sector differs extensively between different countries, depending on such factors as their population and geographical size; their culture and traditions; whether they are developed, emerging or developing economies; the nature of their government and the extent to which government is centralised or devolved. There are some common features that help to define 'the public sector', as illustrated in Figure 1.2, which identifies seven main aspects of public sector activity, including central, regional and local government, defence forces, non-elected public bodies and nationalised industries.

The structure of government in many countries seems to be under a constant process of review. In Scotland, for example, local government was comprehensively restructured twice in 21 years (1975 and 1996); then the devolved Scottish Parliament, within whose policies local government is now required to work, was introduced in 1999. In England, the traditional two tier structure of local government has been reviewed on a phased basis across different parts of the country, with single tier unitary authorities replacing many historic former county and district councils. Also in the UK, much of the structure of the National Health Service has been reviewed on a regular basis over the past 20 years or so.

In more rural areas of Japan, town and village councils have been encouraged to merge or to work more closely together on a voluntary basis. In Denmark and Sweden, the structure has been rationalised

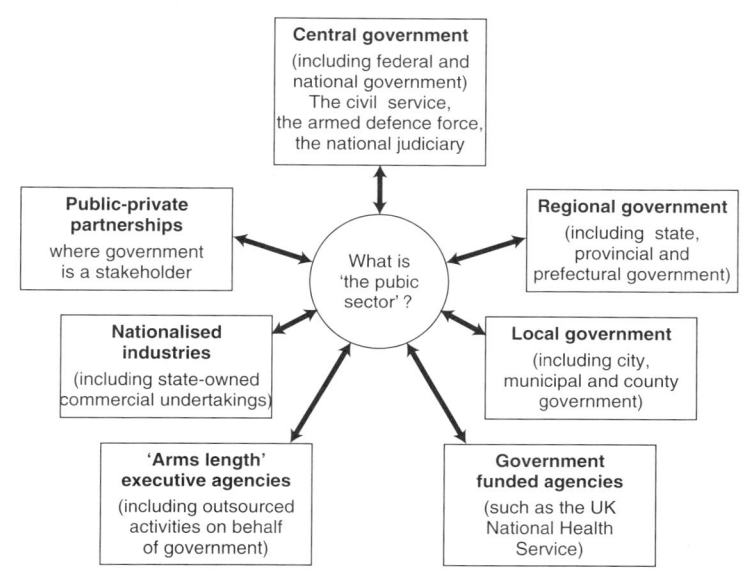

1   A challenging subject for challenging times   *21*

```
                    ┌─────────────────────┐
                    │  Central government │
                    │ (including federal  │
                    │ and national govt)  │
                    │  The civil service, │
                    │the armed defence    │
                    │force, the national  │
                    │      judiciary      │
                    └─────────────────────┘
                              ↕
┌──────────────────┐                    ┌──────────────────┐
│  Public-private  │                    │Regional government│
│   partnerships   │      ╱───╲         │(including state, │
│ where government │ ←── │What │ ──→    │   provincial and │
│  is a stakeholder│     │ is  │        │    prefectural   │
└──────────────────┘     │'the │        │   government)    │
                         │pubic│        └──────────────────┘
┌──────────────────┐     │sector│       ┌──────────────────┐
│   Nationalised   │ ←── │  ?  │ ──→   │ Local government │
│    industries    │      ╲───╱         │ (including city, │
│(including state- │                    │  municipal and   │
│owned commercial  │                    │county government)│
│   undertakings)  │                    └──────────────────┘
└──────────────────┘
┌──────────────────┐                    ┌──────────────────┐
│  'Arms length'   │                    │   Government     │
│executive agencies│                    │ funded agencies  │
│(including out-   │                    │ (such as the UK  │
│sourced activities│                    │  National Health │
│ on behalf of     │                    │     Service)     │
│   government)    │                    └──────────────────┘
└──────────────────┘
```

Figure 1.2
Seven aspects of 'the public sector'
© Dr Peter Smart

into a smaller number of larger councils at county and municipal level.

In many countries, services such as rail, bus and ferry transport, and the supply of clean water have been transferred either into the private sector, under such programmes as the privatisation of the water industry in England and Wales, or the franchising of rail services in Sweden. Aspects of education and the health service have been transferred to quasi-public organisations, such as the *free schools* movement in Sweden and *charter schools* in the USA. In China and the former Soviet states, where there used to be little or no private sector, an increasing proportion of the industrial and commercial base has been or is being transferred to a growing private sector. In Baltic States, such as Estonia, formerly part of the Soviet Union, the process of privatisation has in many respects rendered the economy imperceptibly different to that of its Scandinavian neighbours.

Every change in structure, such as the merger of existing public organisations or the re-allocation of service delivery from the public to the private sector is a challenge for all of those involved. Senior managers are expected to continue to run the service for the benefit of its customers. Employees face the uncertainties of working for a new organisation, potentially under a new management style and regime. Customers may be uncertain as to how the new structure of delivery will meet their needs.

The implications for the HR practitioner are manifold, as they assist with the development of new organisational structures; seek to ensure the smooth transfer of employees to a new organisation; develop new rewards systems and work with line managers on revised performance criteria; and deal with any consequential lay-offs of staff. The pressure on HR practitioners is therefore to develop the requisite competencies of organisation design and development, performance management, negotiation with employees and their trade unions, and employment law. They also require leadership skills and the sensitivity to engage with employees and others as they seek to implement politically-inspired policies.

Challenge 3:
Continuing uncertainty over the state of the global economy
The third challenge is the current state of global, regional and national economies, and the impact that such factors as economic growth, inflation and recession can have on the public sector, and consequently on the management of the people employed by the sector. Very few economies and business sectors have escaped the challenges posed by the recent global recession, widely described as *the worst in over 60 years*. Many developed economies have had to respond by increasing government borrowing, in order to provide financial support to critical business sectors, such as banking and manufacturing.

At the same time, many governments have suffered reductions in tax revenues as incomes and sales have dropped, meaning that there has been a reduction in tax revenues available to spend on traditional public services.

In the same way, regional and local economies have shrunk as citizens have had less disposable income to spend on retail and discretionary items, such as new cars, travel and dining out. Individual businesses have been adversely affected, sometimes leading to business failure which itself reduces the tax base for the locality.

The UK coalition government elected in 2010 indicated that no service, other than the National Health Service and international development, was immune from potential budget cuts. As a result of its comprehensive spending review, announced in October 2010, individual services have been required to plan for substantially reduced budgets, with the expectation that more than 500,000 public sector jobs will disappear over the following four years.

Governments in Greece, Italy, Portugal and Spain have similarly prepared plans for substantial budget reductions, in some cases leading to industrial action by public servants. The US government has forecast record levels of government debt, as a consequence of providing financial support for industry. A number of individual state and local governments in the USA have temporarily been effectively bankrupt, unable to meet the regular pay bill for public servants.

The underlying message is that the affects of the recession will continue to impact on the public sector for some years to come, as governments plan to reduce their budget deficits. It has been accepted that, whereas the private sector adjusted quickly to the new financial reality, the public sector is going to suffer even as economies come out of recession. Politicians and senior managers in the public sector, and their human resource management advisers, need therefore to develop a keen awareness of the potential impact of the continuing challenging economic background on the services that they deliver and the need for innovative pro-active human resource strategies. Strategies might include a freeze on pay increases or reductions in pay, reviews of staffing levels, downsizing, the greater use of new technologies, retraining and reskilling to encourage greater flexibility in the jobs that employees can do, outsourcing of some services to commercial organisations, partnering with other public sector bodies and so on. Many of these, and other, strategies will be referred to in later Essays in this book.

In this regard, the reference to innovative human resource strategies is important: it is better to have plans that are able to meet a range of potential contingencies rather than to adopt a knee jerk reaction to sudden changes in the economy. However, it is appreciated that, in realistic terms, this is not always possible, as when a global economic crisis arising from problems in the international financial sector confronts governments with little or no warning.

Challenge 4:
The impact of technology on the public sector

The wide range of technological developments of the past five decades has helped the public sector become increasingly cost efficient and effective. Many of the more conspicuous developments have been in the administration and management of the public sector, such as the availability of on-line systems for the assessment and payment of taxes, the use of the internet to promulgate information about individual public bodies and their activities, and the use of information and communications technology (ICT) for internal administration. Applications in other areas of activity, from ticketing on public transport to telemetry for monitoring the stock of water in reservoirs, tend more to relate to jobs previously undertaken by craft and manual workers. And of course, specialist aspects of the public sector, such as hospital services, police forensic services and university research departments, increasingly have access to highly specialist technologies.

The introduction of so-called *new technology* has not always been without difficulty, particularly when employees feel their jobs might be at risk or believe that they are entitled to more pay as reward for additional training or using new systems of work. Experience has also shown that the introduction of new or different technology into an organisation frequently requires the hire of employees with different knowledge and competencies, or the development of new skills sets amongst existing employees, thus providing yet more challenges to the management of the people employed in the public sector.

The pace of change in this area seems at times to be exponential, and those responsible for HRM within the public sector need themselves to be able to keep pace with these changes and their implications for organisational design, reward systems, training and development and, in unionised environments, their potential for challenge to the established order of employer/employee relations. They also need to be able to judge how ICT can assist with the delivery of their own services, using systems and processes of what is called *e-hrm*.

Challenge 5:
The changing demography
The demographic make-up is changing in many countries. For example, many parts of the northern hemisphere have an ageing population and a falling birth rate, where the proportion of the population over the normal retirement age is now greater than that below the age of 16. This applies in the UK, where in mid-2009 more than 15% of the population was over 65 whilst fewer than 15% was under the age of 16 (Office for National Statistics, http://www.statistics.gov.uk/CCI/nugget.asp?ID=6), and average life expectancy is increasing by one year every four years. In Japan, some 20% of the population is now over 65. In China, the introduction of the *one child policy* some

30 years ago is creating a similar demographic.

In such countries, increased life expectancy will have a major impact on public health and social care services, including the need to resource them in terms of knowledge, skills and support staff. The incidence of Alzheimer's and dementia will place increasing strain on public health and welfare services. In the UK alone, there are more than 800,000 people with Alzheimer's or dementia (or nearly 1.5% of the total population) (Alzheimer's Research Trust, 2010), forecast to rise to more than one million by 2025. Public policy makers will need to determine the best strategies to cope with such trends, including appropriate HR strategies for the recruitment, training and deployment of staff and joined up thinking between agencies at national and local level, including not for profit support organisations.

By stark contrast, in some parts of the southern hemisphere, such as sub-Saharan Africa, the incidence of HIV/AIDS, malaria and rates of infant mortality have actually caused a rapid reduction in life expectancy over the past two or three decades. For example, it is reported that average life expectancy in Botswana has reduced from 75 before the AIDS epidemic to a forecast 27 years for a child born in 2010 (International Aids Conference, 2002). A similar situation pertains in a number of other countries bordering South Africa. These countries now face the triple dilemmas of increasing demand for health care, a reducing labour force amongst the adult population capable of engaging in long-term economic activity, and a greater proportion of orphans in society. They are amongst the poorest nations in the world and have never had the resources to provide anything like the levels of public service expected in most parts of the northern hemisphere, but rely very substantially on help from NGOs and international aid.

The challenges posed by demography go beyond this brief assessment of the changing age profiles of different nations and the impact that they might have on public services. As the profile of a population changes, so the proportion of the population who are of working age also changes. The proportion of the population of nations such as the UK, Spain, Italy and Japan who are of working age is reducing for three reasons: the increasing emphasis on continuing education beyond normal school leaving age; the desire of some of the population to retire early to pursue other interests; and the impact of more effective birth control methods, which has led to an actual reduction in the numbers of people born most years since the 1960s. Overall, the effect is to reduce the number of people who are available for work.

There are a number of potential solutions to address this problem. The first, which is being actively pursued in the UK and some other countries, is to increase the retirement age for receipt of state pension on a gradual planned basis from the current 65 for men and 60 for women, and to offer incentives to continue working beyond what is now called the default retirement age by increasing their pension when they do retire. The second potential solution is to encourage part-time working, flexible working, job sharing and tele-working from home, in the expectation that some people who might not otherwise be willing to work may choose to join the labour market, or to become returners to work.

A third solution is to permit immigration into the country, to facilitate recruitment to jobs which are otherwise difficult to fill. To give a public sector example, the UK National Health Service has traditionally recruited medical and nursing staff from outside the UK to supplement local labour, and the Australian health service does the same. One Japanese example of labour immigration is in the automobile industry, where a number of the major car companies recruited from countries such as Brazil. During the current economic downturn, many of these workers and their families are unemployed and the local public sector is having to provide support for them, as in Shizuoka Prefecture and Toyota City.

A more critical challenge already alluded to is that which applies in countries such as Botswana, where the average life expectancy is reducing to the point where the so-called average person may have no more than 10–15 years of economically active life beyond school leaving age before they might expect to die. The impact of HIV/AIDS and other causes of premature death has a gravely adverse effect on the number of people within the community who are available for work and to meet all the demands of the labour market.

To conclude this section, it is pertinent to note that UNDESA, in its *World Public Service Report 2005* (which is worth reading for its wider relevance to HR in the public sector) noted that *major socio-economic challenges are posing serious questions about the sustainability and integrity of key aspects of public sector human resource systems* (UNDESA, 2005:4) and then continued that *prominent amongst those challenges with a direct impact on human resource management are demographic shifts, trends in labour migration, including the so-called 'brain drain', and the impact of HIV/AIDS on labour markets and public services, especially in sub-Saharan Africa* (UNDESA, 2005:35), reflecting what has just been written in Challenge 5.

Challenge 6:
Environmental challenges
The sixth challenge is environmental, including the threat of global warming, the need to control air, water and other forms of pollution, the imperative to develop sustainable and renewable sources of energy, and the demand for a continuous clean water supply to the whole population. Much of this agenda is within the remit of the public sector in many countries, including monitoring of noise and atmospheric pollution, the supply of clean water and the removal and treatment of garbage, toxic waste and sewerage, even if the ac-

tual service delivery is outsourced or in some other way undertaken by private enterprise. The refinement of such services will inevitably impinge on the ability of the public sector to recruit and deploy those with appropriate skills and competencies, especially in countries with growing populations and a trend towards greater urbanisation.

The increasing international emphasis on the environment will thus impact on employment in the public sector, from supra-national strategy setting level such as the United Nations and the European Commission, to municipal level where local government is responsible for the collection and disposal of garbage.

Challenge 7:
The increasing pace of change within the community as a whole
The final challenge effectively flows from challenges 1 to 6. This is the increasing pace of change within the community as a whole and within the public sector more specifically. This process of continuous change will require elected and appointed officials with the skills, knowledge and capacity to develop new ways of working and to lead and manage the change process, including the people management skills to motivate their subordinate staff to respond positively to what many see as a constant process of externally imposed change within the public sector.

Other factors affecting employment in the public sector
These seven challenges are perceived currently as the main ones affecting HRM in the public sector across the globe. But this list is not exhaustive. Other factors that the HR practitioner needs to bear in mind include the extent to which employment legislation encourages or restricts flexibility in the employment of public servants; national, regional and local labour markets, and the availability of employees with the required knowledge and competencies; and the culture and tradition within which the public sector operates, from historic democracies, such as those existing in the UK, the Scandi-

navian countries and the Netherlands, to more recently developed democracies and continuing single party states.

A final word:
Unlocking the human potential for public sector performance

It is naturally for the reader to assess the extent to which these various challenges impact on HR in their own context and to identify the strategies that might most effectively respond to them. The thesis of this book is that, even in the most straitened of times, the public sector can deliver quality, cost effective services to its citizens, if it develops innovative strategies that enable it to engage competent and dedicated public servants. This thesis reflects that of UNDESA Report Number 5 which quotes the late Dag Hammerskjöld, former Secretary General of the United Nations, as follows, *fundamentally, man is the key to all problems, not money. Funds are valuable only when used by trained, experienced and devoted men and women* (UNDESA, 2005:iii).

These trained, experienced and devoted men and women, the present author suggests, are the kind who are able to get to grips with economic and political uncertainty, changes in demography, speed of change in information and communications technology, changing labour markets and global concerns over the environment. The challenge for the HR practitioner is to develop and implement the strategies that will facilitate their engagement.

References

Alzheimer's Research Trust, (2010). *Dementia 2010: A report prepared by the Health Economics Research Centre, University of Oxford for the Alzheimer's Research Trust,* Alzheimer's Research Trust, Cambridge, at http://www.dementia2010.org/reports/Dementia2010Full.pdf)

Barzelay, Michael (2001) *The New Public Management: Improving Research and Policy Dialogue*, University of California Press

Beer, Michael, Spector, Bert, Lawrence, Paul R, Qinn Mills, D and Walton, Richard E, (1984). *Managing Human Assets: The Groundbreaking Harvard Business School Program*. The Free Press, New York

Fowler, Alan (1975) *Personnel Management in Local Government* Institute of Personnel Management, London

Gershon, Sir Peter (2004), *Releasing resources to the front line: Independent review of public sector efficiency*, Norwich, HMSO, at http://www.hm-treasury.gov.uk/d/efficiency_review120704.pdf

International Aids Conference, Barcelona, (2002). *Aids cuts life expectancy to 27*, reported in *The Guardian*, 8 July 2002, at http://www.guardian.co.uk/world/2002/jul/08/research.medicalscience

Local Leadership Programme (2010) *Total Place: a practitioner's guide to doing things differently*, Local Leadership Programme, London, at http://www.localleadership.gov.uk/totalplace/wp-content/uploads/2010/03/Total-Place-a-practitioners-guide-to-doing-things-differently.pdf)

Office for National Statistics (2010), UK government statistic, at http://www.statistics.gov.uk/CCI/nugget.asp?ID=6, used under the terms of UK Open Government Licence v1.0

Osborne, David and Gaebler, Ted, (1992). *Reinventing Government*. Addison Wesley Publishing Co, Reading MA

People Management, 1 July 2010 *HR must provide better value for money, warns Met's Tiplady*, editorial

People Management, 6 May 2010 *A cut above*, Jane Pickard

People Management, 6 May 2010 *The insider's view*, anonymous

United Nations Department of Economic and Social Affairs (UNDESA), 2005. *Unlocking the human potential for public sector performance*. United Nations, New York, at http://unpan1.un.org/intradoc/groups/

public/documents/UN/UNPAN021616.pdf

www.ksg.harvard.edu, the website of the Kennedy School of Government, Harvard University

www.kwansei.ac.jp/english/graduate/g_iba.html, the website of the Institute of Business and Accounting, Kwansei Gakuin University, Japan

www.improvementservice.org.uk, the website of the Improvement Service for Scottish Local Government

www.ipma-hr.org, the website of the International Public Management Association for Human Resources (USA)

www.ppma.org.uk, the website of the Public Sector People Managers' Association (UK)

Essay 2

MODELS AND MAPS OF HRM

Aims of Essay 2
By the end of this essay, readers should be able to
- explain a number of models and maps of HR taken from international research;
- assess the application of these models to the arrangements for HR in organisation(s) with which they are familiar;
- identify the cross cultural challenges of the various models.

Models and maps of HR
There is no single universally accepted model of HR. Rather, there is a number, developed in the USA and Europe, each of which reflects HR in a different way. The earliest models widely cited in academic papers were those developed by teams at the Harvard (Beer *et al*, 1984) and Michigan Business Schools (Fombrun *et al*, 1984) in the early 1980s. Subsequently European researchers such as Guest (1987), Brewster and Larsen (1992) and Buyens and de Vos (writing in Brewster and Harris, 1999) sought to determine whether the models developed in the USA were of universal application, or whether there were any peculiarly European perspectives to HR that required the development of a different model.

Much more recently, the UK Chartered Institute of Personnel and Development (CIPD) has developed an HR Profession Map (CIPD, 2010), described *as a comprehensive view of how HR adds the greatest sustained value to the organisations it operates in, now and in the future.*

Each of these models takes a different perspective, but each of them reflects in some way what Holbeche (2009:10) describes in tabular form as *the changing role of HRM*, as illustrated in Table 2.1. This compares the traditional roles of the *personnel function* with the emerging roles of HR, where for each of the traditional roles identified there is a corresponding new role for HRM. As organisations take steps along the road from traditional personnel to strategic HR, they may display a blend of traditional and emerging characteristics.

Traditional roles of the personnel function	Emerging roles of HRM
Reactive	Proactive
Employee advocate	Business partner
Task focus	Task and enablement focus
Operational issues	Strategic issues
Qualitative measures	Quantitative measures
Stability	Constant change
How? (tactical)	Why? (strategic)
Functional integrity	Multi-functional
People as expenses	People as assets

Table 2.1
The changing roles of HRM
(Source: Holbeche, (2009:5), © 2009, Roffey Institute, reproduced with permission)

In addition to the models and maps of HR developed in the USA and Europe, there are other approaches to HR that more closely suit the traditions and cultures of, for example, Japan and China, where the so-called Anglo-Saxon influence on management has until the past two decades or so been less apparent. More recently there has been what has been called the *Mcdonaldisation* of management, an assumption that management concepts and practices developed in the USA have a global application, in the same way as the *big Mac* has become instantly recognisable across the globe (Ritzer, 1993 and 1998).

The aim of this essay is to reflect on a number of these models and maps, how they integrate HR with its surrounding environment and how they may be applied in different cultures and types of organisation, most particularly of course in the public sector. There is also a brief assessment of some of the culturally-specific approaches to HR in the countries of Eastern Asia. No one model or approach is commended over the others, for each has a different set of nuances, but readers may be able to find one or more models that resonate more closely with the way in which HR is approached in their own organisation or from their own cultural background.

The American Models
The models developed by researchers at Harvard and Michigan were the first attempts at creating models of HR. For this reason they tend to be the most widely cited in literature and teaching and to have more visibility than those developed elsewhere. For the purposes of this essay, the Harvard Model will be examined, as one that puts the role of HR into its social and environmental context.

The Harvard Model of HRM
The Harvard Model of HRM (or, as it is formally described by Beer *et al*, 1984, *a map of the HR territory*) is constructed as a systems diagram, demonstrating the contextual relationship between HR, the external environment in which it operates and the internal organisation which it serves. For copyright reasons it has not been possible to include a copy of the complete *map* in this book, but the simplified diagram at Figure 2.1 seeks to offer an impression of the questions raised by the model. A copy of the complete map may be viewed in Beer *at al*, 1984, as well as in a number of other HR publications, including Pinnington and Edwards, 2000 and Armstrong, 2007. At the time of writing, a copy was also available for reference in an on-line version of Armstrong, 2007 – see References at end of Essay.

Whilst the model may at first sight appear complex, it is simple to navigate through the various stages, starting with an assessment of the external factors (or *situational factors*, as Beer *at al* call them) that shape HR policy. These include the legal and economic environment within which the organisation is operating, its labour market

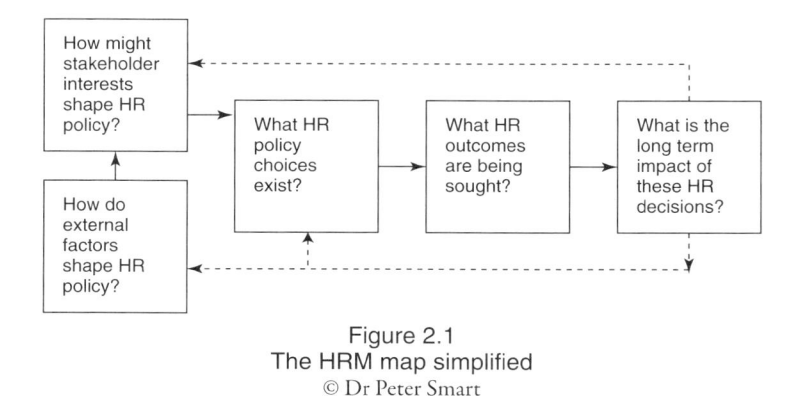

```
┌─────────────┐
│ How might   │
│ stakeholder │ ◄ ─ ─ ─ ─ ─ ─ ─ ─ ─ ─ ─ ─ ─ ─ ─ ─ ─ ─ ─ ┐
│ interests   │
│ shape HR    │ ┌─────────┐   ┌─────────┐   ┌──────────┐
│ policy?     │→│ What HR │ → │ What HR │ → │ What is  │
└─────────────┘ │ policy  │   │ outcomes│   │ the long │
     ▲         │ choices │   │ are being│   │ term     │
┌─────────────┐ │ exist?  │   │ sought? │   │ impact of│
│ How do      │ └─────────┘   └─────────┘   │ these HR │
│ external    │→    ▲                       │ decisions?│
│ factors     │     │                       └──────────┘
│ shape HR    │ ◄ ─ ┴ ─ ─ ─ ─ ─ ─ ─ ─ ─ ─ ─ ─ ─ ─ ─ ─ ─▼
│ policy?     │
└─────────────┘
```

Figure 2.1
The HRM map simplified
© Dr Peter Smart

and the attitude of the trade unions to which it relates. It is also critical to take account of the interests of the various stakeholders, which for the public sector include internal stakeholders such as employees, management and the political structure, and external stakeholders of which the public served by the organisation are clearly important.

Taking account of these factors and interests, the organisation is able to examine the HR policy choices that are available to it, and to identify the HR outcomes that it is seeking to achieve. Beer *at al* identify the policy choices as *employee influence, human resource flow, reward systems* and *work systems*, and the *HRM outcomes* as *commitment, competence, congruence* of the aims of the organisation and its employees and *cost-effectiveness*. As Pinnington and Edwards (2000:6) explain, these are general issues that managers must attend to regardless of whether the organisation is unionised or not, whatever management style is applied, and whether the organisation is growing or in decline.

In terms of the present book, issues of employee influence, commitment and the convergence of employer and employee interests are examined in Essay 8, *Employee relations and engagement*. The concept of human resource flows, into, through and out of the organisation are covered in Essay 3, *Strategic insights and solutions*, which includes an examination of the importance of work force planning. Issues of work systems and cost-effectiveness are examined in Essay 4, *Organisation design and development*, and reward systems are part of Essay 7, *Performance and reward*.

The policy choices and outcomes are as pertinent to the public sector as they are to the commercial sector, particularly as the public sector is increasingly encouraged through New public Management and related concepts to become more commercial in the ways in which it operates.

If the organisation is able to get all the factors identified in the Harvard model into balance, they should lead to long term benefits, for the individual employee in terms of their personal well-being, for the organisation in terms of its effectiveness, and for the well-being of society affected by the organisation's activities. In the case of the public sector, where activities are generally presumed to be to the long term well-being of society as a whole, this consequence is perhaps more obvious than it might be with some parts of the private sector. In conclusion, according to the Harvard model, the impact of its HR decision making extends well beyond the organisation itself. These long term consequences are then used as feedback loops as part of the continuous review of HR policy choices and outcomes – see the dotted lines on the diagram.

Reflection on the Harvard Model
The Harvard model probably remains more widely-known globally than any other model. Even though it has been the subject of academic criticism, its relative universality has never been usurped. Even the most groundbreaking of subsequent research has never managed to achieve the same level of citation, by academics or practitioners. On the other hand, it is suggested by the present author that the nature of the *external factors that shape HR policy have changed substan-*

tially since the mid-1980s, and so a revised set of such factors could be adduced for the 21st century.

For example, changes in the demographics of many countries, the changing economic times and the speed of development of technology, all of which have a major impact on employment in the public sector, could feature in a reworking of the model.

There are challenges arising from the Harvard model for HR in the public sector. It suggests that those engaged in HR at the more senior levels need to monitor a range of external factors, including the impact of the economy on public sector services; political decision making of a strategic nature; case studies and benchmarking exercises on how other organisations in the public sector are achieving cost effectiveness; and developments in technology that might assist the public sector in continuing quests for efficiency. Throughout the organisation, there needs to be an understanding of how HR policy choices and systems should coalesce for the cost-effective achievement of organisational objectives.

The European Models

A number of European models have been developed over the past 20 years or so, of which three are summarised to illustrate the differences in approach.

Guest's model of HRM

David Guest, a UK academic, developed what might be described as a European iteration of the *HR Policy Choices* identified in the Harvard model. His model (1987) is set around seven *policies for identifying human resource and organisational outcomes*, as shown in Table 2.2.

These seven policy areas form the basis of the *human resource outcomes* and the *organisational outcomes* that Guest believes will arise.

Policies	Human resource outcomes	Organisational outcomes
Organisational and job design		High job performance
Policy formulation and implementation / management of change	Strategic planning/ implementation	
Recruitment, selection and socialisation	Commitment	Successful change
Appraisal, training and development	Flexibility/ adaptability	Low turnover
Manpower flows – through, up and out of the organisation		Low absence
Reward systems	Quality	Low grievance level
Communication systems		High cost-effectiveness, ie full utilisation of human resources

Table 2.2
Guest's model of HRM
(Source: Guest D E, 'Human Resource Management and industrial relations', *Journal of Management Studies (1987)*, 24. 5. September, pp.503–21, Table 11, p516 (reproduced with permission))

The most obvious similarities between Guest's model and Harvard are *organisational and job design, reward systems and manpower flows – through, up and out of the organisation.*

The nearest equivalent in Guest's model to Harvard's *employee influence* is *communication systems. Policy formulation and implementation/management of change; recruitment, selection and socialisation;* and *appraisal, training and development* have no direct equivalents in Harvard, although clearly no organisation can expect to have an effective set of HR strategies without underpinning policies, effective recruitment and selection, appraisal and development, or the implementation and management of change. It is in trying to assess the outcomes of these various policy options that Guest's model does not make specific reference to the external and internal environments within which HR is operating, although Guest observes elsewhere that HR *comprises a set of policies designed to maximize organizational integration, employee commitment, flexibility and quality of work* (Guest, 1987:503).

In an era where the public sector across the world is being expected to *do more with less*, Guest's model has some key indicators as to the areas of HR on which public organisations might concentrate: organisational and job design for high performance; recruitment, selection and socialisation for successful change; appraisal, training and development as a key to lower turnover; and achieving appropriate human resource flows to achieve low levels of absence.

Buyens and de Vos model of HR

The second European model was developed by Dirk Buyens and Ans de Vos, academics at Vlerick Leuven Gent Management School in Belgium (in Brewster and Harris, 1999:31–47). Their model is described as the *added value model* of HR in strategic decision making. Briefly, this model introduces two variables: *HR roles*, referring to

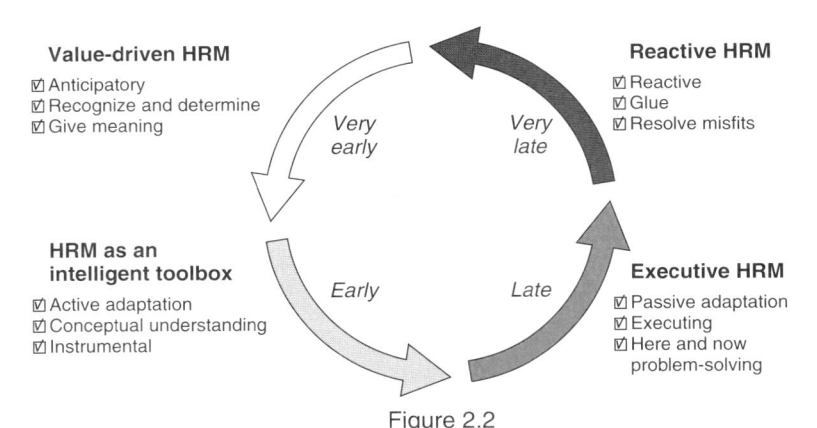

Value-driven HRM
- ☑ Anticipatory
- ☑ Recognize and determine
- ☑ Give meaning

Very early

Reactive HRM
- ☑ Reactive
- ☑ Glue
- ☑ Resolve misfits

Very late

HRM as an intelligent toolbox
- ☑ Active adaptation
- ☑ Conceptual understanding
- ☑ Instrumental

Early

Late

Executive HRM
- ☑ Passive adaptation
- ☑ Executing
- ☑ Here and now problem-solving

Figure 2.2
Buyens and de Vos Value-added Model of HRM
Involvement of HRM in decision-making processes
(Source: Buyens and de Vos, writing in Brewster and Harris (eds) 1999, Reproduced by kind permission of the authors)

2 Models and maps of HRM   *41*

the areas of activity in which HR can add value, and *HR positions*, which assesses the degree of involvement of HR in decision-making. The model stresses the need for HR to be present at all levels of decision-making for, as Brewster and Harris (1997:12) explain, an HR function which only works at the strategic level will be seen to lose much of the value it might add to the organisation. On the other hand, one that operates only at the administrative level will be seen to provide an incomplete service for the strategic business needs of the organisation.

This model is illustrated diagrammatically by three complementary cycles, highlighting the involvement of HR in the business decision-making process (Figure 2.2), the added value of HR at different moments of involvement in decision-making processes (Figure 2.3), and an integrated model for the added value of HR (Figure 2.4), respectively.

The model identifies four roles for HR within an organisation, described respectively as *value driven, intelligent toolbox, executive HRM*

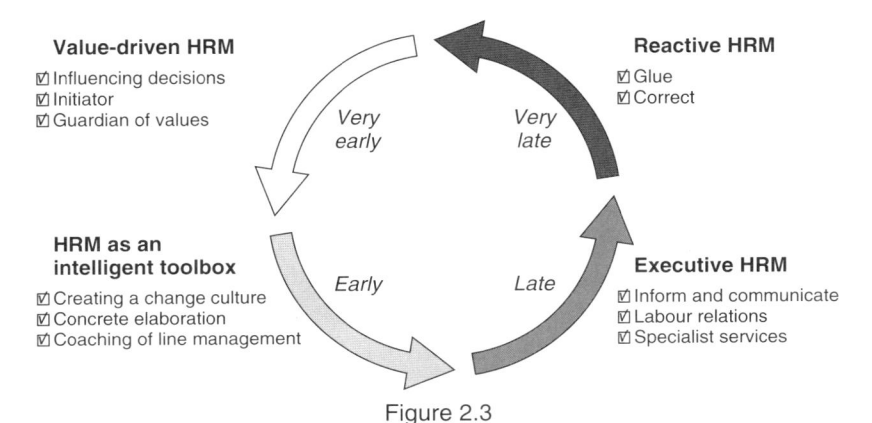

Value-driven HRM
- ☑ Influencing decisions
- ☑ Initiator
- ☑ Guardian of values

Reactive HRM
- ☑ Glue
- ☑ Correct

HRM as an intelligent toolbox
- ☑ Creating a change culture
- ☑ Concrete elaboration
- ☑ Coaching of line management

Executive HRM
- ☑ Inform and communicate
- ☑ Labour relations
- ☑ Specialist services

Very early — Very late — Early — Late

Figure 2.3
Buyens and de Vos Value-added Model of HRM
The added value of HRM at different moments of influence in the decision-making process (Source: Buyens and de Vos, writing in Brewster and Harris (eds) 1999, Reproduced by kind permission of the authors)

and *reactive HRM*. *Value-driven HRM* anticipates issues before they arise, based on the knowledge and perceptions of the HR professionals of the organisation and its environment. It is in on development of strategies in support of the aims of the organisation at the outset and is thoroughly proactive. *HRM as an intelligent toolbox* will be active in developing change management strategies, able to create a change culture through the coaching of line management, and is also in on change management processes early in the programme.

By contrast, *executive HRM* will assist with implementation of change and have a competence in *here and now problem-solving*. It will help the organisation communicate the need for change and how it will be achieved. It will be concerned for the labour relations aspects of decision-making; but it will not be seen as taking any initiative of

Figure 2.4
Buyens and de Vos Value-added Model of HRM
An integrated model for the added value of HRM
(Source: Buyens and de Vos, writing in Brewster and Harris (eds) 1999, Reproduced by kind permission of the authors)

its own. Finally, *reactive HRM* ensures that correct procedures are adopted.

Buyens and de Vos do not suggest that there is a *right* or *wrong* style of HR: rather, HR needs to be a balance of all four of these approaches. As they observe (in Brewster and Harris, 1999:36), *if the HR professional wants to add value to the decision-making process, an anticipative, value-driven style is not sufficient. An active presence in the whole change process is necessary, whereby each role demands specific aptitudes that allow the HR professional to recognise and fill in the opportunities of each position*. In other words, HR should simultaneously be value-driven, an intelligent toolbox, executive and reactive, at appropriate moments in the decision-making process.

Reflections on European models

European researchers have sought to identify whether there are characteristics in European HR that require a different set of approaches to those of the main US models. Sparrow and Hiltrop (1997:201) expressed the view that, *if European management exists, it is in terms of greater cautiousness, sophistication of methods and pursuance of elitist reward and career systems*. Writing a year later in Mabey *et al* (1998:69), they concluded that European managers and academic researchers needed to appreciate four major sets of factors:

1. cultural factors, such as national understandings of distributive justice and manager-subordinate relationships;
2. institutional factors, including the scope of labour legislation and social security provisions and role of trade unions;
3. differences in business structure and system, such as the degree of state ownership and fragmentation of industrial sectors;
4. factors relating to the roles and competence of HRM professionals.

Putting these points into a wider international perspective, there is no doubt that HR in, say, Japan or China will reflect different local cultural factors, even within such headings as distributive justice and manager-subordinate relationships, where factors such as respect for seniority and what Hofstede (1980) described as the *power distance relationship* will dictate a different approach to people management generally compared with the USA or Europe. Indeed, even within Europe there are different cultural factors at play in the Mediterranean nations than there are in northern Europe and Scandinavia. It is thus pertinent to question whether in the decade or more since these European models were promulgated, there have been changes in European society and management that would require a re-examination, in the same way that the present author has suggested that factors within the Harvard model need to be updated.

The CIPD HR Profession Map
The CIPD HR Profession Map is the most recent of the European models being reviewed, having been launched in 2009 (CIPD, 2010). The Map is portrayed as a three dimensional model, bringing together ten professional areas of HRM, three clusters of behaviours and four bands of professional competence (see Figure 2.5). It seeks to capture what HR people do and deliver across every aspect and specialism of the profession and it looks at the underpinning skills, behaviour and knowledge that they need to be most successful. In many respects, it brings together a number of the critical factors of some of the models already assessed.

The development of the Map was a strategic choice on the part of the CIPD to redefine the nature of HR in the second decade of the twenty first century, including the levels within organisations at which HR is practised and the knowledge and behaviours needed to discharge the function effectively. It was developed following an extensive review of the global HR profession and an in-depth investigation involving detailed interviews with HR directors across all the main sectors of the UK economy, as well as many senior professionals and academics. According to the CIPD (2010), it is intended that the Map will set new foundations of best practice in the HR profession, by combining the highest standards of professional competence with alignment to organisational goals, to deliver sustained performance. If this aim is achievable, then the Map should, it is suggested, at least be persuasive in cultures and traditions outside the UK.

The ten professional areas describe what the HR practitioner needs to do and what they need to know for each of these ten areas, at four levels of professional competence. Each of these four levels is defined in terms of their relationship with client departments. The

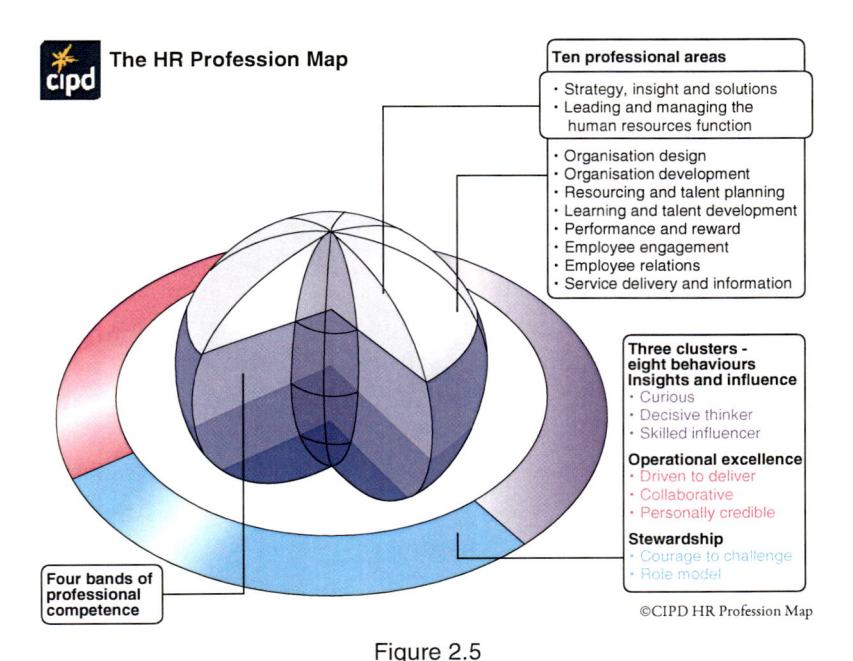

The HR Profession Map

Ten professional areas
- Strategy, insight and solutions
- Leading and managing the human resources function
- Organisation design
- Organisation development
- Resourcing and talent planning
- Learning and talent development
- Performance and reward
- Employee engagement
- Employee relations
- Service delivery and information

Three clusters - eight behaviours
Insights and influence
- Curious
- Decisive thinker
- Skilled influencer

Operational excellence
- Driven to deliver
- Collaborative
- Personally credible

Stewardship
- Courage to challenge
- Role model

Four bands of professional competence

©CIPD HR Profession Map

Figure 2.5
The HR Professional Map
(with the permission of the publisher, the Chartered Institute of Personnel and Development, London (www.cipd.co.uk))

first is the provision or support, service and information, where the focus of activity is on administration, client support and processing activity. The second is at adviser level, where activity is led by specific issues. This involves advising on and managing individual or team-based HR issues and problems. The third level is defined as consultant or cooperative partner, where the focus of activity is on leading the professional area, addressing medium and longer term HR challenges at organisational level. The fourth level is defined as leadership colleague, client confidante and coach. Here, the focus of activity is on leading the function or professional area, developing organisational strategy and related HR strategy and partnering with the client. In public sector terms this last level is likely to be at head of department level and in outsourcing terms it would be the head of the outsourced activity or account manager for the firm to which the outsourced contract has been awarded.

The first of the ten professional areas relates to strategic *insights and solutions*, underscoring the need for more senior HRM practitioners to have a deep understanding of their organisation's activities, strategies and plans, the needs of customers and employees, and of the barriers to sustainable performance. The CIPD (2010) emphasises that practitioners need unique insights to drive organisational performance through the creation and delivery of HR strategy and solutions. It offers examples of key topics included within this professional area, including understanding the external context within which the organisation operates, the levers that drive change, how to identify when change is on the horizon and its potential impact on the organisation, and the skills to help the organisation's leadership team to define an effective response. Each of the ten professional areas is supported by similar statements.

The Map has a number of features in common with the other models reviewed. There is emphasis on the relationship between HR in an organisation and the organisation's strategy and aims. There is reflection on the HR choices and outcomes available to the organisation, although the way in which they are categorised differs between the models. And there is a focus on the complementary levels of HR within the organisation, and a conclusion that each of these levels needs to be present for the effective discharge of the HR function.

Since the CIPD Map has so much in common with the other models reviewed, it will be used as the basis of the structure of Part Two of this book, which examines the various functional elements of HR through a series of six essays. These include indicators of where to find out more about good practice in the public sector, on an international basis.

Asian perspectives on HR

In order to extend the international perspective of this study, some of the characteristics more specific to HR in the Asian context are now briefly examined. These are influenced by tradition and culture, including Confucianism and Daoism, and the balance between ying and yang (see Zhu and Warner, writing in Harzing and van Ruysseveldt 2004:195–217).

They cite, for example, the concept of *workplace is family* in China, which requires organisations and management to look after the interests of fellow employees, while employees have a high commitment to the organisation. Building on this concept of family, HR practices such as teamwork, sharing values and information, and group-oriented incentive schemes are based on the foundation of collectivism, and are prevalent in Japan and other Asian societies as well as in China.

Japanese characteristics of HRM

The model of HR in Japan that has operated in the economy generally since the early 1960s has been based on *three pillars* of life-time employment, a seniority-based wage scheme, and enterprise trade unions (Zhu and Warner, 2004:201), and on the philosophy of collectivism, although there have over the past ten years or so been signs of changes to these traditional approaches.

The pillar of life-time employment is enshrined in law for many public servants (Jichi Sogo, 1995), and the traditions of seniority-based wage schemes and seniority-based promotions are common-place in the public sector. The philosophy of collectivism is reflected in Japanese HR practices, through such group-oriented traits as teamwork and team decision-making, and the payment of group, rather than individual, bonuses. Acculturation of this kind will inevitably affect such aspects of HR as organisation design, resourcing and talent planning, and performance and reward.

Zhu and Warner (2004), the Jichi Sogo Centre (1995) and other specialist writers point to slow but perceptible changes in the traditional HR systems in Japan, arising from the major recession that the country experienced from 1990–2001. Organisations, including in the public sector, are increasingly recruiting mid-career professionals and technicians to do specific jobs, alongside a reduced programme of generalist recruitment. Seniority pay is slowly being replaced in some sectors by performance-related and skill/knowledge-based pay, with some emphasis on individual incentives, and promotion schemes are gradually changing from age and seniority-based to one that reflects employees' capabilities and leadership traits.

Chinese characteristics of HR
The final reference in this chapter is to HR in the People's Republic of China, to provide a perspective from a socialist market economy point of view where, from 1949 to 1979, just about the whole economy was in the public sector. Following the introduction by Premier Deng Xiao-ping of the *open door* policy to encourage international investment and foreign trade, employment practices have developed as part of the transition to a mixed economy, in which foreign en-

terprises and joint ventures and locally-owned private companies are operating alongside the public sector and the remaining state-owned enterprises.

Prior to the introduction of the open door policy, as Zhu and Warner explain (in Harzing and van Ruysseveldt, 2004:209), employment and labour relations were epitomised by a number of so-called values of Socialist Superiority, collectively summed up by the term the *three irons*: the *iron rice bowl* (*tie fan wan*) referring to life-time employment (Warner, 2008:774); *iron wages* referring to the fixed wage system, and the *iron chair*, being the inflexible relationship between cadre and manager. Once employed, the state provided all the main requirements for living, which effectively shackled the individual to the state owned enterprise or ministry for which they worked. This, in conjunction with the principle of *hukou*, or place of registration, more or less ruled out any chance of labour mobility from enterprise to enterprise or from one location (place of registration) to another.

Since 1979, government initiatives have sought to reform wages, employment, welfare and management. The principle of *distribution according to work* has sought to motivate employees by linking individual performance, skills and status with income, including variations in reward based on productivity, and the reforms have sought to encourage greater mobility of labour, although evidence suggests that this has been harder to achieve in the state sector than in the growing private sector.

A more western form of human resource management (*renli ziyuan guanli*, literally *labour force resources management*) is gradually taking its place in Chinese organisations, although state owned enterprises are more inclined still to practise old style *personnel management* (*renshi guanli*), according to Zhu and Warner (in Harzing and van Ruysselveld, 2004:210). Their conclusion is that even in larger Sino-foreign joint ventures, HR tends to be more inward looking on more mundane aspects of HR, rather than engaging in strategic HRM. There is, therefore, no homogenous model of HR in Chinese enterprises, rather, as Warner (2008:777) writes, a hybrid of old style personnel management with an increasing element of HRM.

Some concluding reflections

A number of common threads are apparent from the analysis of the US and European models, whilst the assessment of the influences of Confucianism and Daoism and of cultural traditions in East Asia begins to explain why the speed and nature of development of models of HR there has been different. What is clear from writers such as Zhu and Warner, is that in East Asia there are signs of hybrid systems of HR in the making. Finally, in the same way that European researchers sought to distinguish specifically European characteristics of HR, so it is appropriate for academics and practitioners in China and Japan, and in other continents, also to discern how cultural traditions might impact on an unquestioning application of US (or European) models to their own circumstances.

References

Armstrong, Michael (2007) *A handbook of human resource management practice*, 10th edition (reprint), Kogan Page, London, at http://books.google.com/books?id=D78K7QIdR3UC&printsec=frontcover&dq=a+handbook+of+human+resource+management+practice&hl=en&src=bmrr&ei=l6Y1Tfq8HdCzhAe30smiCw&sa=X&oi=book_result&ct=result&resnum=1&ved=0CCgQ6AEwAA#v=onepage&q&f=false, page 7

Beer, Michael, Spector, Bert, Lawrence, Paul R, Qinn Mills, D and Walton, Richard E (1984) *Managing Human Assets: The Groundbreaking Harvard Business School Program*. The Free Press, New York

Brewster, Chris and Harris, Hilary (1999) *International HRM: contemporary issues in Europe*, Routledge, London

Brewster, C and Larsen, H (1992) 'Human Resource Management in Europe: Evidence from ten countries', *International Journal of Human Resource Management*, Vol 3, No 3, pp.409–434

Buyens, D and de Vos, A (1999) writing in *International HRM: Contemporary Issues in Europe*, eds Brewster C and Harris, H, Routledge, London

Centre for European Human Resource Management at Cranfield School of Management – see www.cranet.org for detailed information

Chartered Institute of Personnel and Development (2010) *HRM Profession Map*, at www.cipd.co.uk/hr-profession-map

Guest, David E (1987) 'Human Resource Management and Industrial Relations', *Journal of Management Studies*. 24. 5. September, pp.503–521

Harzing, Anne-Wil and van Ruysseveldt, Joris (eds) (2004) *International Human Resource Management*, SAGE Publications, London

Hofstede, G (1980) *Culture's Consequences: International Differences in Work-related Values*. Sage, Beverly Hills, Ca

Holbeche, Linda (2009) *Aligning Human Resources and Business Strategy*, 2nd ed, Butterworth-Heinemann, Oxford

Jichi Sogo Centre (1995) *Local Public Service Personnel System in Japan*, Jichi Sogo Centre, Tokyo,

Mabey, Christopher, Salaman, Graeme and Storey, John (1998) *Strategic Human Resource Management: A reader*, Sage, London

Pinnington, Ashly and Edwards, Tony (2000) *Introduction to Human Resource Management*. Oxford University Press, Oxford

Ritzer, George, 1993 *The Mcdonaldisation of Society* Pine Forge Press, Los Angeles

Ritzer, George, 1998 *The Mcdonaldisation Thesis*, Sage Publications, London

Sparrow, P.R., Hiltrop, J-M (1997), 'Redefining the field of European human resource management', *Human Resource Management*, Vol. 36 No.2, pp.201–26

Sparrow, P.R., Hiltrop, J-M (1998) *Redefining the field of European Human Resource Management: A Battle between national mindsets and forces of business transition?* writing in Mabey, Christopher, Salaman, Graeme and Storey, John (eds) (1998) *Strategic Human Resource Management: A Reader*, Sage/The Open University, London

United Nations Department of Economic and Social Affairs (2005) *Unlocking the Human Potential for Public Sector Performance: World Public Sector Report 2005*. United Nations, New York

Warner, Malcolm (2008), 'Re-assessing human resource management 'with Chinese characteristics': an overview', *The International Journal of Human Resource Management*, Vol. 19, No. 5, May 2008, 771–801, Routledge, London

Zhu, Ying and Warner, Malcolm, *HRM in East Asia*, writing in Harzing, Anne-Wil and van Ruysseveldt, Joris (eds) (2004) *International Human Resource Management*, SAGE Publications, London

Introduction to Part 2

Part 2 consists of six relatively short essays. Each examines one or more current challenges for a particular aspect of HR.

The titles of the essays follow closely eight of the ten professional areas of HR, as identified in the CIPD HR Professional Map (the other two areas are covered by Essays 9 and 10, in Part 3 of the book).

The aim of this Part is to highlight and examine some of the critical issues confronting HR in the public sector today. These include the requirement for the reshaping of familiar public organisations, consequent upon the current financial constraints; the need for organisations to recruit and develop high potential employees, who have the professional competencies and political skills to lead the public service through the current period of adversity into a rebirth of efficiency and cost effectiveness; and the development of salary schemes that reward performance rather than length of service and possibly even mediocrity.

In the space available, it is unfortunately not feasible to provide a detailed exposition of all the challenges facing HR, or indeed to describe case examples in depth. Instead, each chapter contains references to publications that contain such examples, as well as to websites from a number of countries, from which further information on good practice might be discerned.

Essay 3

STRATEGIC INSIGHTS AND SOLUTIONS

Aims of Essay 3

By the end of this essay, readers should be able to

- confirm the importance of developing human resource strategies in the public sector;
- explain the kinds of strategic insights that are needed for HR in the public sector to make an effective contribution to the successful operation of their organisation;
- demonstrate their ability to help find strategic solutions to the challenges facing the public sector.

Introduction

'Now is the most exciting and challenging time in the history of HR.' With these words, former US vice-president Al Gore addressed the 2010 annual conference of the US Society for Human Resource Management (SHRM, 2010). He encouraged HR practitioners to lead their organisations by focusing on the long-term challenges (Smedley, 2010a), adding, 'Increasingly, the most important challenges business faces today are in the realm of HR.'

These thoughts will be encouraging to practitioners who are keen to respond to the kinds of challenges identified in Essay 1. They also direct the mind to the strategic nature of HR, as examined in Essay 2. After all, how can an organisation plan for the longer term without aligning their organisational and HR strategies? The key is not just having the right strategy, but having the right number of people with the right knowledge and competencies to achieve the organisation's strategy.

The thesis of this essay is that for HR practitioners in the public sector to be effective, and accepted as adding value to the organisation, they must first focus on working with politicians and senior managers in the development of innovative HR solutions that respond to the challenging times in which they are working. It is in this way that they can, as Gore suggests, lead their organisations by facing the long-term challenges. The essay first addresses what the author sees as three key questions that affect the ability of HR to develop strategic insights and deliver strategic solutions. It concludes by examining the role that *HR* (or *Workforce*) *Planning* serves as an underpinning tool of HR strategy.

Three key questions
Three questions arise in relation to HR practitioners in the public sector. First, are they ready, willing and capable of responding to the kind of challenge that Gore has laid down? Second, are the politicians, who are ultimately accountable to their constituents for delivering an effective public sector, prepared to allow HR to take the kind of leading role that Gore identified? And third, just how can the public sector develop strategic solutions when the world in which it operates is so volatile and unpredictable?

Ready, willing and capable?
Only the individual practitioner can fully and honestly answer the first key question. So how can they judge? They might ask themselves a number of questions. For example, do they have a deep understanding of the organisation, its activities, strategies and plans? Do they know the drivers of and barriers to sustainable performance, and the needs of customers and employees? How can they develop unique insights to help drive business performance through the creation and delivery of HR strategy and solutions?

Ulrich (1998) suggested that organisational success springs from capabilities such as speed, responsiveness, agility, learning capacity and employee confidence (*People Management*, 1998). Research at the UK's Roffey Park Management Institute (cited in Holbeche,

2002:111) suggested practitioners need to develop high-level political influencing skills, strategic thinking, IT skills and financial awareness, as well as entrepreneurial skills and creative thinking. These, the research concluded, could be developed through a mix of training, mentoring, peer coaching, challenging assignments and learning review processes. Campbell (quoted by Smedley, 2010b) advises that HR needs to *react faster and be more flexible*. He observes that HR is often slow and restricted by policy. Unless policy is linked to a company's values or legal requirements, HR needs to be flexible and fast.

These four brief references give some clue as to the capabilities that are required of senior HR practitioners in the public sector. The question practitioners will need to ask themselves is, 'how well do I measure up against these various criteria?' After all, they are much more high level than the constituent skills and knowledge of a more basic grade HR practitioner. In the terms of Buyens and de Vos (1999), these are the capabilities required for operating at the level of *value-driven strategic partner HRM* (see Essay 2). Or, in the words of the CIPD HR Profession Map (CIPD, 2010a), they require the courage to challenge, to be a role model, to be a curious, decisive thinker and to be a skilled influencer.

These attributes tend to be over and above the formal education programmes, at graduate or postgraduate level, offered to those wishing to become HR practitioners. Such programmes are understandably designed for those establishing themselves in a career in HR. They are to ensure as far as possible that practitioners are able first to function effectively at the operational level. Some practitioners choose not to plan their career beyond that level, and there is no shame in that. But for those who do aspire to the more influential levels of HR, the attributes identified by CIPD, Ulrich, Campbell and others need to be developed. Inevitably, perhaps, much of this learning will be on the job and through programmes of coaching and mentoring; at the academic level, an MBA or MPA programme might be appropriate.

One debate that has taken place in the UK professional journal *People Management* (People Management, 2010) is whether the most senior appointments in HR should actually be held by those who have received specific training in the profession, or whether they might more aptly be held by those with a background in a functional aspect of business. The latter, it is claimed, tend to be strategic and more flexible in their thinking rather than procedural and rules-based, financially numerate and focused on results, able to help drive sustainable organisational performance. In the public sector, an appropriate analogy might be between the merits of, say, the generalist approach of the UK civil service or Japanese local government, where officials gain experience in a number of functions or services as part of their career development, and that of UK local government, where senior HR managers have tended traditionally to be appointed on the basis of their professional experience and background. Either way, the emphasis in this essay is on the capacity of such managers to offer strategic insights on, and solutions to, the HR challenges faced by their organisations.

The relationship between politicians and the HR function

At first sight, one might conclude that it is only the politicians, who are ultimately accountable to their constituents for delivering an effective public sector, who can decide whether they are prepared to allow HR to take a leading role in reviewing and implementing organisational strategies. However, HR practitioners should not overlook the personal and professional responsibility that they have for demonstrating that they have the critical attributes to work with politicians and the senior management of operational services as they develop strategies for changing times.

At the local level they need to establish their credibility with the ultimate decision takers. Holbeche (2002:17) talks of the paradox that prevents some HR functions from making strategic decisions. If their basic procedures are not in good order, they may not be considered capable of higher level operations. Yet those who concentrate on administration are seen as reactive and a cost to the organisation. One way of resolving the paradox, she suggests, is by taking good care of routine responsibilities through ICT so that the function can concentrate on high added-value activities, by orienting the function to a more strategic approach.

At the national level, there are various organisations that are able to help promote HR on a professional basis. The CIPD in the UK and SHRM in the USA are obvious examples of professional associations representing HR across the full spectrum of the economy. The International Public Management Association for Human Resources (IPMA-HR) in the USA and the Public Sector People Managers' Association (PPMA) in the UK are specific to the public sector. Both have as part of their mission the development of practitioners who are able to demonstrate their fitness to participate on equal terms with operational colleagues in strategy development.

The objectives of the PPMA include raising the profile of the people management function in the UK public sector and leading the development of and commitment to best people management practice. It seeks to influence and contribute to the development of public policy and legislation in this respect, constantly advocating the need for higher standards of people management and development to further enhance the delivery of public services (http://www.ppma.org.uk/pages/default.aspx and http://www.ppma.org.uk?pages/about.aspx)

Amongst its wide range of membership services, the IPMA-HR (http://www.ipma-hr.org) offers a programme entitled Developing Competencies for HR Success. This requires candidates to demonstrate amongst other criteria their *understanding of the organization's mission, vision, and values, and the business plan for execution using these attributes as its foundation for meeting the organization's service goals, and their ability to link specific human resource initiatives to the greater organization's mission and service deliverables* (http://www.ipma-hr.org/professional-development/certification/competencies).

In Japan, institutions such as the Japan Intercultural Academy of Municipalities play a similar role by providing short courses that raise the profile of HR in the public sector (JIAM, 2009:7).

Developing strategy in a volatile and unpredictable world
It is inevitable that many engaged in the public sector will question the wisdom of trying to develop organisational and HR strategies for a volatile and unpredictable world. 'How', one might ask, 'can we plan when budgets may be cut by 5%, 10%, 25%, even 40%? And how can we meet customer expectations for public services if we have to cut the number of employees?' It cannot be denied that planning against such uncertainties is difficult. But it is better to develop a range of possible ways forward that try to take account of various scenarios, than to have no plans at all. This proposition will be taken further later in this essay, in the examination of HR (or Workforce) Planning.

Strategic insights and strategic solutions
So what kinds of strategic insights does the HR practitioner require, to help the organisation achieve high levels of sustainable performance with reduced levels of resources (what is often described as 'doing more with less')? There are insights extrinsic to the HR function and those that are intrinsic to it. Some of the extrinsic insights have already been referred to: an ability to articulate the kinds of challenges examined in Essay 1; an understanding of the organisation, its activities, strategies and plans; the reasons for and means of delivery of the range of services that the organisation is responsible

for; and the ability to watch what is going on in the wider world and assess the impact it might have on the organisation. An aptitude for articulating this appreciation will do much to convince the organisation of the contribution that HR can make outside its formal functional sphere.

The intrinsic insights relate more specifically to the HR function itself: the development of workforce planning and strategies for recruiting, managing, developing and rewarding talent; and the ability to relate the people needs and structures of the organisation to the internal and external labour markets. Such insights also imply knowledge of employment legislation and of the factors that motivate and engage people at work; the establishment of networks through which the organisation is able to benchmark its activities against those of similar organisations; and the ability to demonstrate competence in a range of HR skills and activities.

The implication is that a practitioner who is able to offer strategic insights is more capable of contributing to the development of strategic solutions in conjunction with other senior management. Here are two scenarios by way of illustration.

Scenario 1: Care for the elderly

One of the services the organisation provides is domiciliary and residential care for the elderly. It is estimated that the number of people requiring such care will increase by 2% a year for the next five years, then at 5% a year for the following five years. The organisation proposes to build one new residential home for 40 residents every four years and to meet the remaining need by providing support to elderly residents in their own homes.

The HR function should be expected to add value to these decisions by working with the operational department to agree the numbers and types of employee required for this expansion in service; to analyse the local labour market to identify the optimum sources of new employees; to prepare phased recruitment, orientation and training plans to ensure the appropriate staff are available to meet service requirements; and to monitor and assess the effectiveness of their plans.

Scenario 2: New ICT system
A new ICT system will enable citizens to submit details of their income and related items for tax purposes, on-line at the end of each fiscal year. Immediately the required information has been submitted, the system will notify the citizen whether they have underpaid or overpaid income tax in the past year. If they have overpaid, the system will initiate a refund direct to their bank. If they have underpaid, the system will generate information as to how and when the balance due will be collected. The system will replace the traditional paper-based system, which required officials of the tax service to input the data to the system and to generate refunds and notices of underpayment. Around 40% of existing posts in tax offices will be declared surplus to requirements. Some staff will be transferred to other jobs or locations; some may be retrained; others may need to be laid off, although the organisation seeks to avoid compulsory lay-offs.

The HR function should work with the operational directors to assess the current staffing complement, including such data as age, length of service, qualifications and experience and career patterns. It should develop a strategy for reducing the number of staff over an agreed timescale, including policies for retraining, redeployment and relocation, and for seeking volunteers for early retirement or redundancy. It should develop means of communicating with employees and engaging them in consultation. Ultimately, one test of the success of the HR input to the process will be achievement of required new staffing levels, with the right knowledge and competencies, motivated to deliver the new system, without disruption by strikes or other industrial action.

HR (or Workforce) Planning

HR, or Workforce, Planning is an essential tool for the successful implementation of any HR strategy. Its purpose may briefly be described as ensuring the *right people, right time, right skills*. It has been defined by the CIPD (2010b:4) as *a core process of human resource management that is shaped by the organisational strategy and ensures the right number of people with the right skills, in the right place at the right time to deliver short- and long-term organisation objectives*. As the CIPD (2010b:2) observe, workforce planning presents an important opportunity for HR to be involved in building the strategic plan for the future of the business. It might even be argued that workforce planning is the starting point for all aspects of people management, as it seeks to define the labour force that is required now and in the future to deliver the products and services that customers demand. However, the CIPD add, while HR practitioners appear to recognise the importance of workforce planning in principle, for many there is what is described as a 'knowing–doing' gap.

There are two internal drivers for workforce planning: *organisational strategy* and *operational requirements*. It is possible to identify many examples of organisational strategies from the public sector: where the local health service decides to close the emergency room in two of its hospitals and concentrate provision in one specialist unit; where the education service is required to build new schools in a new town area; where a city council agrees to outsource its financial processing services to a private company; and where a police authority is required by central government to respond to a cut of 15% in its income. Similarly, it is possible to suggest any number of examples of operational requirements from the public sector, particularly in the emergency services, such as police and fire, where levels of cover 24/7 are critical, or from the caring services, where agreed staffing levels of medics, nurses and carers are essential.

There are also two external drivers: *customers and stakeholders* and *market forces*. Customers of the public sector have expectations of their service providers: warm clean properly staffed schools for their children, or highways that are maintained to a high standard after adverse winter conditions. Public opinion can have a huge impact, on such issues as public sector pay, job reductions the council is making – even, where the public sector is politicised, whether there is a change of power at election time, which affects public sector strategy. Market forces include such factors as social trends and labour market issues. Financial pressures may require parts of the public sector to forego at least some of their traditional role as service providers, to concentrate on the purchase of more cost efficient services from the third sector and commercial organisations.

No apology is made for the nature of the examples in these paragraphs. They have been chosen to illustrate the array of issues of which senior HR practitioners in the public sector need to be aware: and the list could go on and on.

Getting the organisational structure fit for purpose
There are two key stages before workforce planning can be effective. The first is the determination of organisational strategy. The other is ensuring that the organisational structure is fit for purpose. The drivers for change and the pace of change have already been highlighted. There is a greater imperative now than at any time in history for organisations to keep their structures under review, with as much built-in flexibility as possible to allow for potential future changes in strategy. The traditional view of the public sector as a static, job-for-life type of organisation has long gone in many countries and employees as well as structures must be willing and able to cope with change. As Prabhu (quoted by Smedley, 2010b) comments, *organisations can develop new ways of producing and delivering their products and services (process innovation), and they can develop new ways of reconfiguring the whole business (business model innovation).*

The workforce planning process

The CIPD (2010c:10) have confirmed the conventional view that there are four stages in the workforce planning process, outlined in Figure 3.1.

The first stage will be influenced by three elements: organisational strategy, people strategy and the operations plan. Next, there must

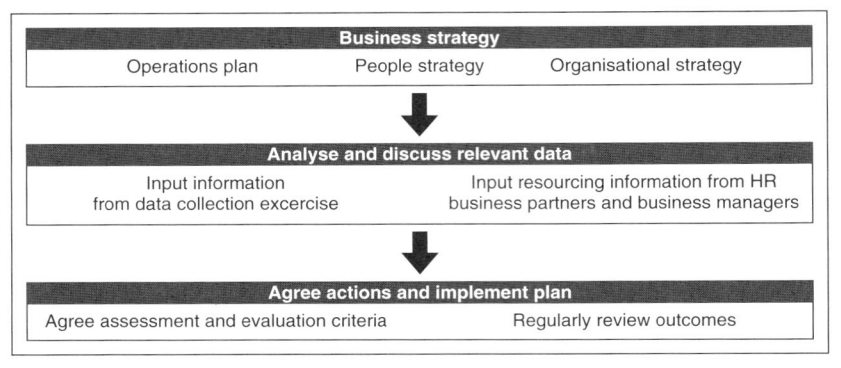

```
┌─────────────────────────────────────────────────────────────┐
│                     Business strategy                        │
│   Operations plan      People strategy     Organisational    │
│                                              strategy        │
└─────────────────────────────────────────────────────────────┘
                              ↓
┌─────────────────────────────────────────────────────────────┐
│              Analyse and discuss relevant data               │
│   Input information              Input resourcing information│
│   from data collection           from HR business partners   │
│   excercise                      and business managers       │
└─────────────────────────────────────────────────────────────┘
                              ↓
┌─────────────────────────────────────────────────────────────┐
│              Agree actions and implement plan                │
│  Agree assessment and              Regularly review outcomes │
│  evaluation criteria                                         │
└─────────────────────────────────────────────────────────────┘
```

Figure 3.1
Process model for business planning
Source: Guide to Workforce Planning
(with permission of the publisher, the Chartered Institute of Personnel and Development, London (www.cipd.co.uk))

be discussion between senior management and HR around the availability of data relevant to the planning purpose. The third stage seeks agreement on what the plan is trying to achieve for review against available resources. This will involve a review of labour supply data, both internal to the organisation and external to it, and a review of the capability of the present workforce to deliver the plan. From this review, it will be possible to identify any gaps between supply and demand: in current financial circumstances this may show a surplus of labour against demand requirements.

The final stage involves developing actions from the analysis of all the data, including recruitment and deployment of labour, how to recognise potential through learning and development, and any consequential review of structures. The type and range of information required for effective workforce planning is illustrated in Figure 3.2.

Workforce planning does not exist in isolation from either the rest

Qualitative-internal
Information from strategic planners - potential new directions, technology scenario planning, new ways of working
Information from senior management - strategic
Information from line managers - operational
Information from HR on people - skills, training needs, attitudes and performance, potential

Quantitative-internal
Workforce data - eg turnover, absence data, demographics, training spend, recruitment spend, working patterns, succession planning, talent planning, competence levels achieved, skills audit etc.
Organisation date - customer information, results of strategic assessments such as feasibility of offshoring or outsourcing, restoring requirements, orders.

Information used in workforce planning

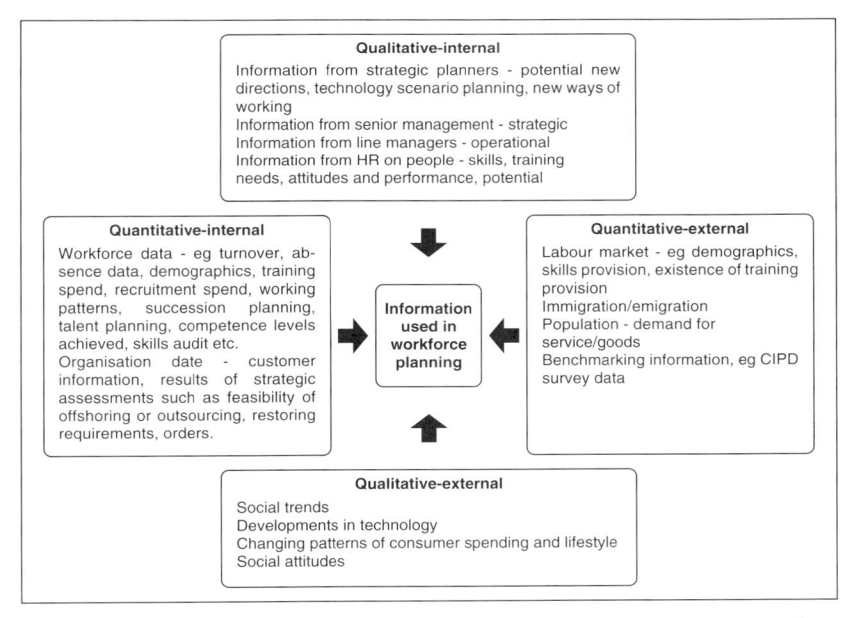

Quantitative-external
Labour market - eg demographics, skills provision, existence of training provision
Immigration/emigration
Population - demand for service/goods
Benchmarking information, eg CIPD survey data

Qualitative-external
Social trends
Developments in technology
Changing patterns of consumer spending and lifestyle
Social attitudes

Figure 3.2
Information used in workforce planning
Source: Guide to Workforce Planning
(with the permission of the publisher, the Chartered Institute of Personnel and Development, London (www.cipd.co.uk))

of the organisation or other aspects of the HR function. There is a shared responsibility between line managers, HR practitioners and specialist planning support staff for the development, implementation and monitoring of the plan, as illustrated by Figure 3.3.

And there should be links with organisation design and develop-

Workforce planning	Organisational owners	Related business planning activity
Determine overall frame and objectives of workforce planning	Board/executive management	Developing organisational strategy with input on people dimension: • business plan • HR strategy • corporate governance • key organisation purpose, aims and objectives
Provide information on future plans and business direction and resource requirements to fulfill them	Senior managers	Develop business plan at unit level • operational plans • input information on cross-organisational resourcing needs
Input information on skills requirements, working time, rostering requirements, resourcing needs	Line managers	Develop departmental plans Communicate team goals and objectives. Input into operations plans
Input people management information and metrics	HR	Translate business plans into local HR plans. Provide expertise and guidance on developing skills, performance and workforce capabilities.
Pull information together and produce draft plans for discussion with all stakeholders	Workforce planning specialists, including data-modellers	Access the business planning process to collect and analyse relevant data

Figure 3.3
Workforce planning roles and responsibilities
Source: Guide to Workforce Planning
(with the permission of the publisher, the Chartered Institute of Personnel and Development, London (www.cipd.co.uk))

ment, resourcing and talent management, learning and talent development and employee engagement.

Workforce planning in uncertain times

The art behind workforce planning is the ability to assess a number of scenarios that might impact on the organisation and to articulate them into HR plans. Conventional wisdom advises preparing what is likely to be the *best case scenario*, the anticipated *worst case scenario* and possibly one or more scenarios between the two.

Thus, if central government has indicated that it anticipates cutting departmental budgets by between 10% and 40% over the coming four years (as happened in the UK in the summer of 2010), the *best case scenario* may be assumed to be a reduction of 10% in budget, the worst case may be 40%, with other scenarios set at indicative levels of 20%, 25% and 30%. In less draconian times, a standstill budget may be seen as a middle course, with potential growth and potential reductions as the best and worst case scenarios.

Figure 3.4 outlines some of the imponderables and challenges that face those engaged in workforce planning and identifies potential ways of overcoming them.

Challenges	Enablers
Lack of clarity on focus in the organisation strategy	A "triangle" of conversation about future requirements between the business, HR and finance
A constantly shifting strategy	Workforce champions in the business
Too much focus on the operational and budgetary planning at expense of longer-term planning or a strategic direction for planning	Having a good process that enables everyone to feed in information and is informed by the needs of the business
Processes that don't join up, meaning information is not fed into the planning cycle or that effort is duplicated	HR and the line working together to understand future people needs
Failure to develop plans that are responsive enough to adapt to a changing environment	Understanding the difference between supply and demand for labour
Failure to reviews plans in the light of new information that indicates change	Bottom-up communication feeding the planning process
Poor-quality datasystems	Good-quality data that people can believe, accompanied by adequate analysis to explain what it means for the business
Too much focus on the numbers of people required and not enough on capacity and potential to develop new skills and abilities in the future	Leaders acting on the data to make informed decisions
An uncomplicated system or trying to do too much too soon	Regular planning cycle and reviews with feedback into the planning process
Lack of planning skills and good guidance on workforce planning	Developing managers' workforce and resource planning skills

Figure 3.4
Challenges and enablers of workforce planning
Source: Guide to Workforce Planning
(with the permission of the publisher, the Chartered Institute of Personnel and Development, London (www.cipd.co.uk))

Sources of information and examples of workforce planning in the public sector

A number of organisations offer information about workforce planning, including case studies of public bodies that have engaged in the activity.

The CIPD is one. Their Guide to Workforce Planning (CIPD, 2010c) includes brief references to planning from a number of UK public bodies and three case studies, taken from a major city council, a police authority and a National Health Service Trust.

In the USA, the IPMA-HR website (http://www.ipma-hr.org) contains various resources and case studies relating to workforce planning (http://www.ipma-hr.org/hr-resources/successful-practices/list-topics/Workforce-Planning), including a copy of the internal guide to workforce planning of a city council (http://www.ipma-hr.org/sites/default/files/pdf/BestPractices/2006WFPDGuide.pdf) and a benchmarking report on workforce planning that contains case studies from across the USA (http://www.ipma-hr.org/sites/default/files/pdf/BestPractices/2009Bench.pdf).

In the UK, the Local Government Improvement and Development Agency in England and Wales (http://www.idea.gov.uk) and the Improvement Service for Scotland (http://www.improvementservice.org.uk) both include workforce planning amongst their advisory and support services. The websites of both organisations offer various support materials and case studies.

Concluding remarks

This essay has sought to address a number of issues key to ensuring an effective relationship between organisational strategy and HR strategy, including the role that workforce planning might play in easing this relationship. It acknowledges that workforce planning in turbulent economic times can be a major challenge, but urges those readers keen to operate at the most senior levels in HR in the public sector to develop the attributes that will enable them to play a leading part in the development and implementation of HR strategy.

References

Chartered Institute of Personnel and Development (CIPD) (2010), *Explore the Map*, at http://www.cipd.co.uk/hr-profession-map/explore-the-map.htm

Chartered Institute of Personnel and Development (CIPD) (2010) *Guide to Workforce Planning*, London, CIPD at http://www.cipd.co.uk/NR/rdonlyres/6367E224-9F4D-4470-95AC-B4F08D701F95/0/5219_Workforce_planning_guide2.pdf

Holbeche, Linda (2002) *Aligning human resources and business strategy*, Butterworth-Heinemann, Oxford

International Public Management Association – Human Resources, home page http://www.ipma-hr.org/ and Competencies Certificate page http://www.ipma-hr.org/professional-development/certification/competencies

Japan Intercultural Academy of Municipalities, home page http://www.jiam.jp/english/index.html and pdf brochure of courses http://www.jiam.jp/english/pdf/jiam2009_e.pdf

People Management, editorial, 11 March 2010

Public Sector People Managers' Association, home page http://www.ppma.org.uk/pages/default.aspx and 'about' page http://www.ppma.org.uk/pages/about.aspx

Smedley, Tim (2010), 'Gore tells HR: "Focus on long term"', *People Management*, 15 July 2010

Smedley, Tim (2010), 'On the up', *People Management*, 22 October 2009

Society for Human Resource Management (2010) 'Gore: Take the long view' web report, at http://www.shrm.org/Publications/HRNews/Pages/GoreTaketheLongView.aspx

Ulrich, Dave, interviewed by MacLachlan, R (1998) HR with attitude, *People Management*, 13 August 1998

Essay 4

ORGANISATION DESIGN AND DEVELOPMENT

Aims of Essay Four
By the end of this essay, readers should be able to
- explain the changing nature of organisation design and development in the public sector;
- assess and propose appropriate organisation designs for public sector organisations that best enable them to achieve their short-term and longer-term objectives;
- identify some of the cultural issues that might impact on organisation design and development.

Introduction
A close relationship between HR and the objectives of the organisation is critical to effective organisation design and development. This will ensure that the structure of the organisation and the design of the jobs within it will contribute effectively to the achievement of the organisation's objectives. The structure of the organisation is also an essential pre-requisite guiding other aspects of the HR function, including recruitment and selection, workforce and succession planning, and learning and develop.

The essay will briefly examine the underpinning principles of organisation design, including some of the developments in design that have been adopted by the public sector over the past 25 years or so. It will assess some of the key steps that organisations should take as they seek to change structures and ways of working, in the context of the challenges facing the public sector. Finally, it will note some of the more radical ideas for discharging traditional public services arising from current political thinking.

Principles of organisation design

As the public sector continues to face the challenges examined in Essay 1, organisations will need to find ways of structuring to ensure that they remain as effective as possible with fewer employees. The principles of organisation and job design will be critical in this situation.

Writers on organisations, such as Fincham and Rhodes (1999), Mullins (2002) and Rollison (2002) identify the key principles of that underpin the design of organisational structures to ensure that they are as far as practicable *fit for purpose*: in other words, are convergent with organisational objectives. Mullins (2002:536) summarises these principles in tabular form (see Table 4.1), which should be read alongside the following notes.

There is a number of key questions that an organisation should ask, whether it is establishing an organisation structure for the first time, or is redesigning its structure for future fitness for purpose, as illustrated in Table 4.1.

What are the organisation's key objectives?

How might it achieve these objectives in the most cost effective and customer focused manner?

How does it deliver customer focused services?

How does it provide 'back office' (or support) services?

In what ways can it best ensure communication within and between services?

How does it ensure that structures are sufficiently flexible and responsive to changes that it cannot yet predict?

Will it be able to resource the structure with people with the required knowledge and competencies?

Table 4.1
Key questions of organisational design
© 2011 Dr Peter Smart

Within each of these key questions rests a number of consequential considerations. Many public sector organisations are complex, required to deliver a range of services to a defined population in a defined area. Even a small relatively remote Japanese village council or French *commun* may be required to provide elementary and high school education, library and cultural services, garbage collection and local highway maintenance. There may be no apparent clear relationship between some of these services, other than that they are all part of the public service to the people who live or work in the village, or travel through it. Thus, it will be appropriate as part of organisation design to articulate the strategic sub-objectives that relate to each of the services, as part of this process. How much more complex, therefore, will be the corresponding process for a Japanese prefecture, an English county or a French *département*?

The next step is to assess how the organisation might structure its services to achieve its objectives in the most cost effective and customer focused way. Cost effectiveness implies so-called *lean* structures, with limited layers of management and supervision, empowerment of front line staff to take decisions within broad organisation policy, and deployment of staff with a broad range of knowledge and competencies able to respond flexibly to a number of tasks. Information and communications technology (ICT) may streamline administration. The introduction of *super departments*, whose directors are accountable for the delivery of a number of functions, might reduce management costs (for example, a directorate of corporate services that includes responsibility for legal, financial, HR and ICT support). The creation of shared services departments between two or more neighbouring public agencies might also reduce the costs of management and of support services.

The ethos of customer service has become increasingly apparent in the public sector over the past decade or two. Such a commitment requires the organisation to *get close to the people it serves*. This might be by having a single *help point* for information and questions about services, having area offices close to housing schemes and shopping malls, offering free phone call centres and engaging the public in the definition and prioritisation of service requirements. In organisation design terminology, it requires consideration of benefits of decentralisation of service delivery and possibly the introduction of matrix organisations (see below).

For the past four decades, line managers in the public sector have been demanding greater transparency in the provision of back office services, such as finance, ICT and HR, asking whether they are receiving value for money for the outcomes achieved against the costs of provision. Recent and current trends in the delivery of support services have included the development of service level agreements that specify the services that will be provided and the associated costs; decentralising some aspects of support service delivery to operational departments; setting up shared services with neighbouring agencies; and outsourcing services.

The relationship of people within and between departments is clearly critical to the smooth and effective operation of any organisation. Four main formal organisational relationships exist, as illustrated in Figure 4.1. The *line relationship* reflects the authority and responsibility of line managers for the activities of their department or section. Authority and control flow vertically down through the structure. The relationship between an employee in a specialist or advisory position and line management to whom they provide a service is described as the *functional relationship*. The *staff relationship* exists for example between a senior manager and his or her personal assistant. The latter has little or no formal authority over other staff but has *representational authority* on behalf of their manager. Finally, the relationship between staff in different departments, so important for the co-ordination of activities and overall organisational performance, is described as the *lateral relationship*.

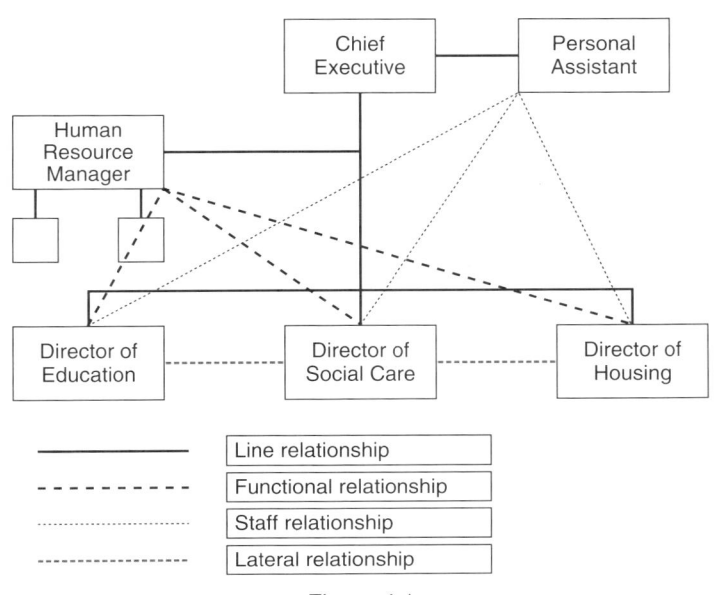

Figure 4.1
Illustration of types of formal organisational relationships
© 2011 Dr Peter Smart

Traditional organisational structures tend to lack the flexibility and speed of response required by organisations facing regular change. *Project teams*, often of a short-term nature, consisting of staff from a range of functions may be established to attain a specific task or clearly defined objective. *Matrix management* (Knight, 1997) also allows greater flexibility in the allocation of resources and the meeting of organisational objectives.

Project teams and matrix organisations are increasingly formed on an inter-agency basis, with one of the public agencies being designated as *lead authority*, responsible for high level management of the project or task – see example in Figure 4.2, an inter-agency arrangement for the care of children with special needs.

```
                    ┌──────────────┐
                    │  Education   │
                    │   Director   │
                    │(Special Needs)│
                    └──────────────┘
```

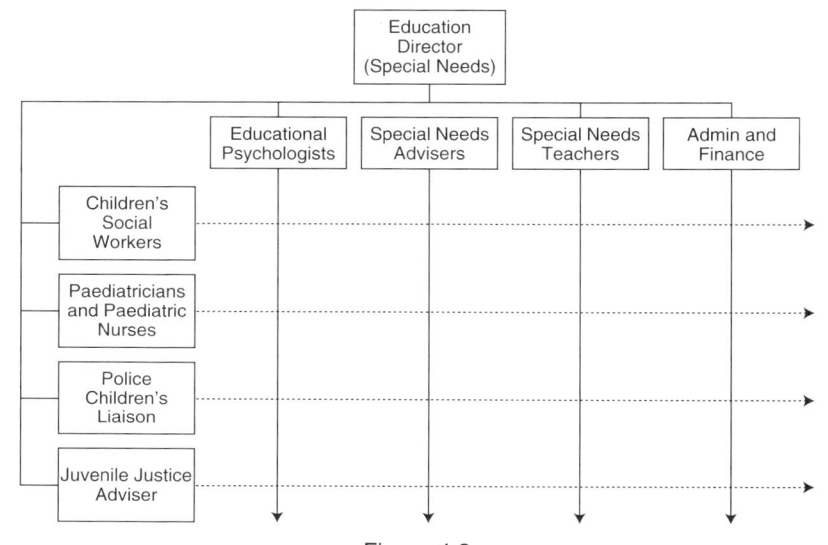

Figure 4.2
Example of service-based matrix organisation structure
© 2011 Dr Peter Smart

This structure can be more difficult to manage, since the staff involved may have divided loyalties, between their principal employer and the matrix team, offering scope for conflict in such issues as time allocation and responsiveness to decisions made.

Challenges for organisation design

The structure of an organisation can never be permanent. It will be appropriate at the date of its approval, but circumstances will change over time. It may portray the ideal situation, presuming that each position is filled by a person who meets all the requirements of the job to be performed. However, some positions may be vacant, their work either not being done or being covered by others as part of their workload. Some may be filled by employees who are still learning aspects of the work. Changes in working practices may demand greater flexibility and multi-skilling on the part of employees, or the introduction of greater delegation by management.

Job descriptions and people specifications need to allow for flexibility to introduce new ways of working, such as flexible working hours, tele-working and working from home. Finally, organisation design must be responsive to the internal and external labour markets within which the organisation operates, including the availability of labour with the required knowledge, qualifications and competencies.

Changing nature of organisational structures

As Fincham and Rhodes (1999:374) comment, *the emphasis in modern structures is on identifying key processes around which to build new networks and multi-functional teams.*

This quest has been made necessary by the movement towards leaner organisations, the demand for greater flexibility and the extension of ICT beyond the office to tasks traditionally undertaken manually. Some of the newer models and approaches are now considered.

Leaner and flatter structures

From around the end of the 1980s, the trend in organisation design towards flatter structures and *leaner management*, has been linked with processes of *downsizing*, by which the numbers of office based employees are reduced, and *delayering*, by which the number of levels in the organisation is reduced. Outcomes include wider spans of control, semi-autonomous work teams and the empowerment of junior positions.

The 'flexible firm' and the 'shamrock organisation'

During the 1980s, two models of flexibility were developed in the UK: the *flexible firm* (Atkinson, 1984) and the *shamrock organisation* (Handy, 1989). Both were developed at a time when, as Atkinson (1984:28) pointed out, there was market stagnation as the result of a world recession; reduction in employment levels; uncertainty about economic growth; increasing pace, and decreasing cost, of technological change; and demands to restructure working time in unconventional ways. It was thus in circumstances similar to those in which the public sector is working today that Atkinson proposed his model of the *flexible firm*.

He suggested that organisations need to look for *functional flexibility*, to allow the rapid redeployment of employees to different activities and tasks; *numerical flexibility*, to adjust the number of employees to match the demand for labour; and *financial flexibility*, so that pay and other employment costs reflect the supply of and demand for labour and permit a shift to new pay and benefits systems.

THE FLEXIBLE FIRM

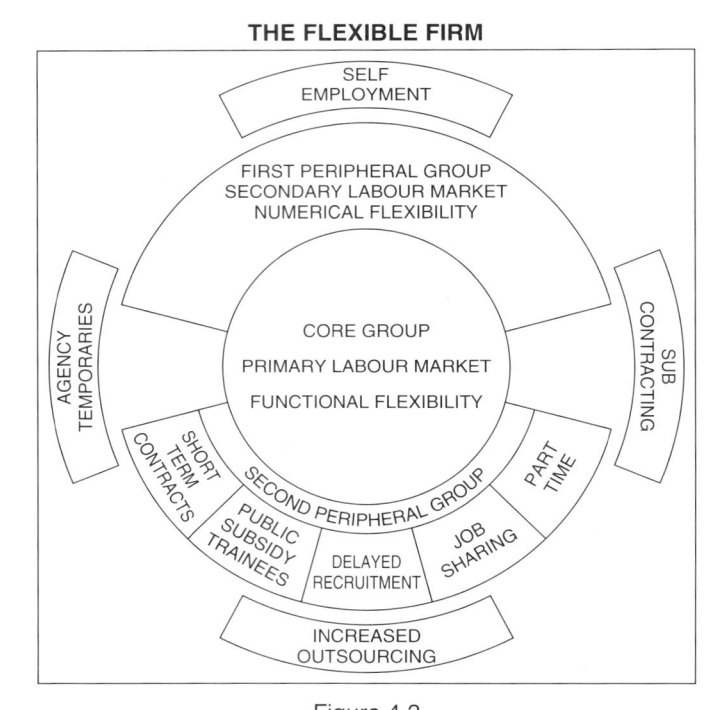

- SELF EMPLOYMENT
- FIRST PERIPHERAL GROUP
- SECONDARY LABOUR MARKET
- NUMERICAL FLEXIBILITY
- AGENCY TEMPORARIES
- SUB CONTRACTING
- CORE GROUP
- PRIMARY LABOUR MARKET
- FUNCTIONAL FLEXIBILITY
- SHORT TERM CONTRACTS
- PUBLIC SUBSIDY TRAINEES
- SECOND PERIPHERAL GROUP
- DELAYED RECRUITMENT
- JOB SHARING
- PART TIME
- INCREASED OUTSOURCING

Figure 4.3
'Atkinson's Model of the Flexible Firm'
(Source: © John Atkinson, writing in Personnel Management, August 1984 Reproduced with kind permission)

Figure 4.3 illustrates Atkinson's *flexible* firm (or *flexible organisation*, in public sector terms), which is largely self-explanatory. The organisation has a central core of full-time permanent career employees, who undertake the organisation's key activities, supported by peripheral and numerically flexible groups of workers.

Handy's (1989) *shamrock organisation* – see Figure 4.4 – has similar attributes, with a professional core of employees supported by a flexible labour force of part-time and temporary workers and a contractual fringe of people from outside the organisation. One main difference between Handy's model and Atkinson's is the diagrammatic shape: whereas Atkinson's is effectively a series of concentric circles, Handy's is based on the shape of the leaf of the shamrock plant.

Both models require a change in traditional management, to include different leadership arrangements for the various elements of the models, ways to maintain the commitment and motivation of employees who are not part of the central core, and a client/contractor relationship.

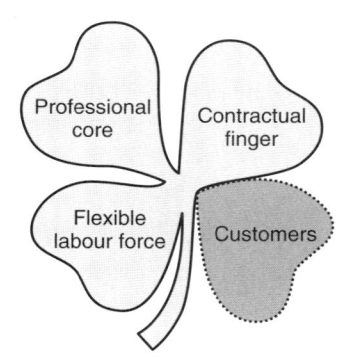

Figure 4.4
Representation of Handy's shamrock organisation

Virtual organisations

The increased use of information and communications technology can permit the development of *virtual organisations*, which may allow some employees to work from home either permanently or for part of their time. Telemetry, mobile telephone technology and other innovations permit peripatetic employees, such as meter readers for public utilities, to record information on hand-held computers, and to download the information through a telephone line at home. Potential problems arising from the development of virtual organisations include questions of control, trust and ensuring the employee undertakes their expected workload as and when it is required to be done. However, new technologies and software allow monitoring of activities as a proxy for direct human supervision.

Business process re-engineering and related systems of improvement

Over the past half century or so, several concepts have been used to streamline management structures, including the Japanese philosophy of *kaizen* (literally, *improvement* or *change for the better*), *total quality management* and *business process re-engineering* (Hammer, 1990). They aim to eliminate waste and provide a better service to the customer. The fundamental review of processes inevitably leads to a consequential review of structures that might involve the reallocation of work, the disappearance of some former jobs and the creation of new ones in their place and the development of new organisational structures.

Job design

Effective job design is an activity that should be consequent on organisation design, to ensure that the organisation makes the best use of the people it employs and to enhance the personal satisfaction they derive from their work. Research over the past 60 years or so suggests that people are much more likely to be motivated by, and take pride in, their work, if they feel they are doing a whole job, with some element of personal discretion as to the scheduling of tasks and the pace with which they may be undertaken. Organisations should ideally allow the employee to make best use of their knowledge and competency, consistent with the objectives of the organisation, and offer training and developmental opportunities for personal growth.

Job rotation, job enlargement and *job enrichment* enable organisations to redesign jobs and provide variety in their work for employees. Job rotation involves moving an employee from one job to another to provide some element of variety in the short term and potentially a wider range of experience in the longer term. Job enlargement involves increasing the scope of the job and the range of tasks that the person carries out, usually achieved by combining a number of related tasks at the same level. Job enrichment attempts to enrich the job by incorporating motivating or growth factors such as increased responsibility and involvement, opportunities for advancement and the sense of achievement.

CHANGE MANAGEMENT

The theme of change permeates this essay. As Paton and McCalman (2000:5) observe, change will not disappear or dissipate. Managers, and the organisations they serve, will be judged on the ability effectively and efficiently to manage change, handling complex change situations over ever decreasing time-scales. On the other hand, the CIPD (2005) reports that over 40% of reorganisations fail to meet their objectives. The following paragraphs illustrate two approaches to change management and organisation development that will assist with the effective implementation of change.

Model of perpetual transition management

This model (Buchanan and McCalman, 1989, cited in Paton and McCalman, 2000:10) – see Figure 4.5 – suggests that managers need to be able to deal with constant change, since it will never be possible to achieve a permanent end state. The model is formed of four interlocking management processes that must take place to implement

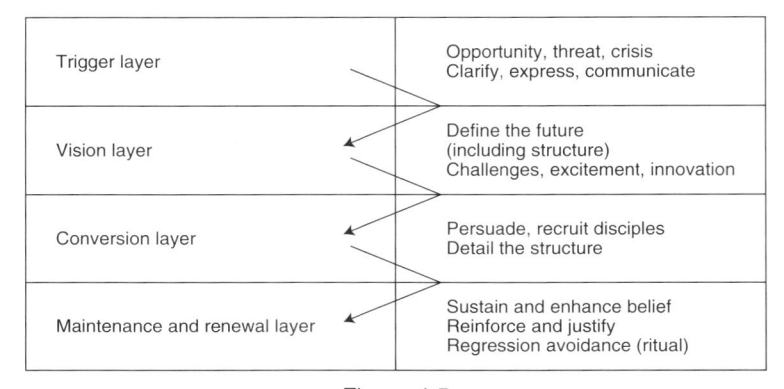

Trigger layer	Opportunity, threat, crisis Clarify, express, communicate
Vision layer	Define the future (including structure) Challenges, excitement, innovation
Conversion layer	Persuade, recruit disciples Detail the structure
Maintenance and renewal layer	Sustain and enhance belief Reinforce and justify Regression avoidance (ritual)

Figure 4.5
Buchanan and McCalman's model of perpetual transition management
(Buchanan and McCalman, 1989:198)
(Reproduced by permission of SAGE Publications, London, Los Angeles, New Delhi and Singapore, from Paton, Robert A and McCalman, James, *Change Management: a guide to effective implementation*, © SAGE 2000)

and sustain major organisational changes:

trigger layer, identifying opportunities for major change, explaining them to stakeholders;

vision layer, articulating a vision of where the organisation is heading, generating excitement in challenges and innovation;

conversion layer, mobilising support in the organisation for the new vision by detailing the proposed new structures;

maintenance and renewal layer, sustaining and enhancing changes through alterations in attitudes, values and behaviours, and avoiding regression to old ways.

Intervention strategy model

This model, illustrated in Figure 4.6, provides a means of managing the change cycle in a structured and logical way. It has three clear phases, definition of the problem or challenge; generation and evaluation of potential solutions; and implementation, and permits iteration to earlier stages in the process as appropriate. To be fully effective,

4 Organisation design and development 83

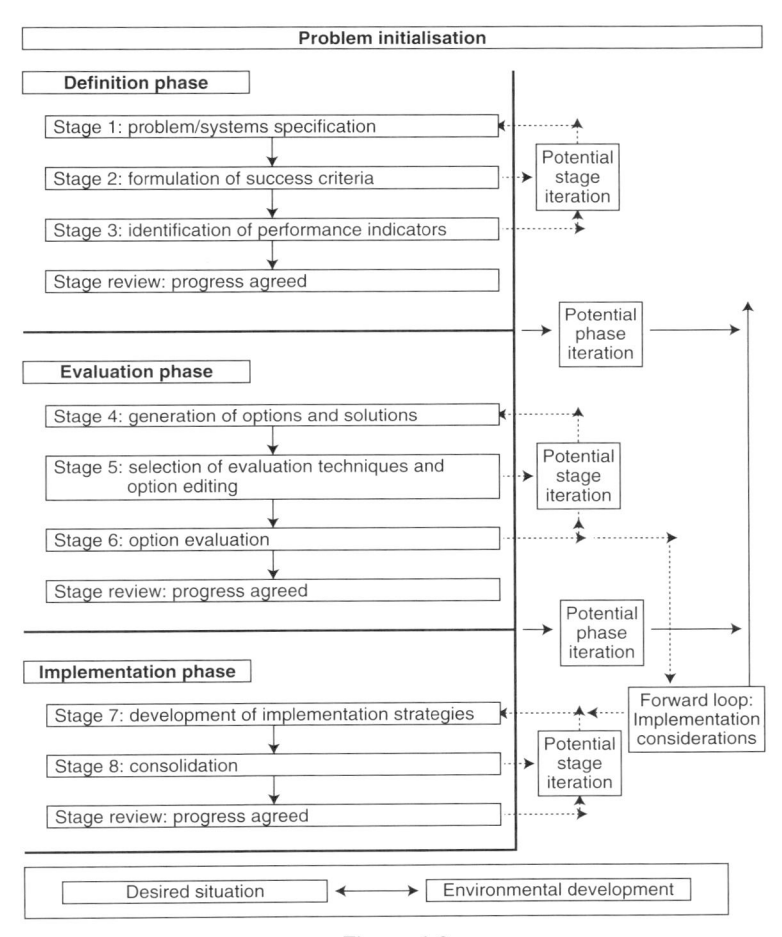

Figure 4.6
The intervention strategy model of change
(Reproduced by permission of SAGE Publications, London, Los Angeles, New Delhi and Singapore, from Paton, Robert A and McCalman, James, *Change Management: a guide to effective implementation*, © SAGE 2000)

the process should be clearly explained to stakeholders and progress through the phases should be regularly communicated. The model should not be used to push through the problem owner's preferred solution as a sham for involvement and engagement of others.

The 'seven C's of change'

This model, proposed by the CIPD (2005), has seven stages:

choosing the right people to participate in the change programme. The role of HR includes championing the people agenda; redefining roles, jobs and skills; adapting and refining HR policies and communicating with employees;

crafting the vision of what the organisation wishes to achieve from change;

connecting changes across the organisation, to ensure that outcomes do not conflict with one another;

consulting stakeholders, to ensure that their views on the proposed change are taken into account;

communicating on a regular, consistent and targeted basis, at each stage of the change;

coping with the change, as well as ensuring the organisation meets its day-to-day responsibilities. This dual responsibility can be the source of enormous stress for many people, particularly if the job or status of the individual is under threat as a result of the proposed change;

capture learning from the change programme that can be used in future.

(reproduced with the permission of the publisher, the Chartered Institute of Personnel and Development, London (www.cipd.co.uk))

Organisation development

Organisation development (OD) is rooted in research undertaken by American behaviourists and psychologists from the late 1940s, who concluded that participation by employees in decision-making led to attitude change, higher performance and greater commitment to the organisation. OD has built on this approach where organisations involve their employees in a planned and systematic approach to enabling sustained organisation performance. It is possible to find out more about OD in a number of sources, including in the CIPD Factsheet on Organisation Development – see References at end of Essay.

OD is undertaken by trained practitioners who help create alignment between different activities, projects and initiatives. It involves groups of people in the organisation to maximise engagement, ownership and contribution. In stressing these aspects of engagement, ownership and contribution, OD as a tool for change moves well beyond the traditional approach taken by some management consultants, who tend to gather information and impressions, then come up with recommendations independent of the people in the organisation.

Holbeche and Cheung-Judge (2009a) argue that it is possible even in a downturn to bring about change and avoid the worst consequences of change by using an OD approach. However, they advise that in a downturn organisations can only absorb or engage in a limited amount of change, so it is important to be clear about the nature of any change perceived as necessary. Then, by securing the engagement of the people likely to be affected by the change, it will have a greater chance of success.

Relationship between organisation design and OD
To complete this brief overview of organisation design and organisation development, it is appropriate to assess the relationship between the two. Holbeche and Cheung-Judge (2009b) explain that organisation design is more conventionally associated with 'technical' top-down aspects of organisational structure and system changes, and that its fundamental premises are about economic rationalisation. By contrast, OD is a distinctive approach to building healthy and effective organisations, by improving the way people work together, using techniques based on behavioural science and process facilitation.

CULTURAL IMPLICATIONS
Organisational change and job redesign may be more difficult to achieve in some cultures than in others, taking into account factors

such as public sector and employment legislation, and the power of trade unions. Cultural attributes, for example, whether there is a tradition of engaging employees in consultation and organisation development activities, may also impact on the ability to implement change speedily and effectively. Yet external forces may require the organisation to change, whether its leaders and employees seek change or not. Indeed, the national governments of many countries are using public expenditure as part of fiscal policy, by imposing cuts in the funding of subordinate public bodies upon whom the actual decisions on restructuring will fall.

It is argued therefore that an understanding of the principles of organisation design and of models of change management are critical for the HR practitioner, as is an appreciation of the HR implications of OD. For now, it is pertinent simply to point out the expectation that employees legitimately have, to be consulted and kept informed of changes that might affect their jobs, their pay and benefits and other aspects of the contractual relationship they have with their organisation. For example, many public employees in the countries of the European Union have statutory rights to be consulted when their employer proposes any such changes. By contrast, their counterparts in Japan will have statutory protection to a job for life unless they volunteer to accept some form of severance or early retirement.

AND YET MORE CHANGE!
The more flexible organisational structures proposed by Atkinson (1984) and Handy (1989), and adopted by the *Reinventing Government* and *New Public Management* movements, have been embraced more or less enthusiastically in the public sector in many countries over the past 20 years or so. Many services have been outsourced on a voluntary basis or exposed to competitive tendering under national legislation. Some public bodies have experimented successfully with *kaizen*, *total quality management* and *business process re-engineering*. Traditional government services have been split between a smaller

policy making unit, centrally located and providing strategic advice to their political leaders, and operational executives responsible for implementing policy. Public utilities in many countries have been removed from the public sector altogether and are now provided by the private sector. Others have been the subject of employee or management buy-out and transfer into the private sector. And there are examples of services traditionally provided by democratically-elected authorities being transferred to the control of appointed boards, whilst remaining publicly funded.

Many of these changes are inspired by political ideology or because the traditional elected organisations are not perceived as sufficiently innovative or willing themselves to experiment with new forms of structure. The development of *charter* schools in the USA and *free* schools in Sweden and the UK, and proposals by the 2010 coalition government in the UK to introduce employee-owned cooperatives as a possible model for public services are more recent manifestations of change. Concurrently, there are indications that both major services such as education or social work and back *office functions*, including HR, of many public bodies will be provided jointly on behalf of a number of neighbouring public bodies in the interests of economy of scale, and that the trend to fewer, larger public bodies will continue to reduce the costs of democracy and management.

There, then, is the challenge for HR, to keep fully up-to-date with such developments, to be responsive to what Al Gore, former US vice-president, described as *the most interesting and challenging time* in the history of the function (Smedley, 2010).

CASE STUDIES
Organisations such as the UK Local Government Improvement and Development (IDeA), the CIPD, the Scottish Improvement Service and US IPMA-HR and similar bodies have advisory notes and information about organisation design and development, and change

management, on their respective websites.

For example, IDeA offers a range of resources on organisation redesign on the following web page: http://www.idea.gov.uk/idk/core/page.do?pageId=15770039,

CONCLUDING REMARKS

Some of the precepts of Atkinson's and Handy's models are present in the public sector in the USA and the UK, Scandinavia and Australia and New Zealand, where competitive bidding and other forms of outsourcing have been introduced over the past 25 years or so, and where the concepts of *Reinventing Government* (Osborne and Gaebler, 2002) and *New Public Management* are present.

Osborne and Plastrik (1997:63) advise that, before an organisation makes structural changes, it must first seek to change the strategy, what they call the *DNA*, of the organisation. They emphasise that whilst *structure is important, bureaucratic structures are a huge barrier to reinventing government*. The point they are making is that there is no point simply in imposing a new structure on an organisation and expecting it to work. Commitment to the principles and strategy behind the new organisation are critical.

References

Atkinson, J (1984) 'Manpower Strategies for Flexible Organisations', *Personnel Management*, vol 16, no 8, August 1984, pp.28–31

Buchanan, D A and McCalman, J (1989) *High Performance Work Systems: The Digital Experience*, Routledge, London

Chartered Institute of Personnel and Development (2005), *HR: Making change happen*, CIPD, London, at http:www.cipd.co.uk/Bookstore/_catalogue/HRPractice/1843981130.htm

Chartered Institute of Personnel and Development (2010) *Factsheet on*

Organisation Development, CIPD, London, at http://www.cipd.co.uk/subjects/corpstrtgy/orgdevelmt/orgdev.htm

Fincham, Robin and Rhodes, Peter S (1999) *Principles of organisational behaviour*, Oxford University Press, Oxford and New York

Hammer, Michael (1990) 'Re-engineering work: don't automate, obliterate', *Harvard Business Review*, 68, Jul/Aug, 104–112

Handy, Charles B (1989) *The Age of Unreason*, Business Books, London

Holbeche, Linda and Cheung-Judge, Mee-Yan (2009) *Organisational development in a downturn*, CIPD, London, at http://www.cipd.co.uk/NR/rdonlyres/6A2B97B9-6BF0-4F98-BE65-D91CA4013418/0/impact_27_linda_holbeche_article_organisational_development.pdf

Holbeche, Linda and Cheung-Judge, Mee-Yan (2009) *Organisational development in focus*, CIPD, London, at http://www.cipd.co.uk/NR/rdonlyres/35F49ABC-0436-40D3-B02B-5B6838CCEEF2/0/Impact_28_org_develop_qanda.pdf

Knight, K (ed) (1997) *Matrix Management: A Cross-functional Approach to Organisation*, Gower, London

Mullins, Laurie J (2002) *Management and Organisational Behaviour*. Pearson Education Limited, Harlow

Osborne, David and Gaebler, Ted (1992) *Re-inventing Government*, Addison-Wesley, Reading MA

Osborne, David and Plastrik, Peter (1997) *Banishing Bureaucracy*, Reading MA, Addison-Wesley

Paton, Robert A and McCalman, James (2000) *Change Management: a guide to effective implementation* (2nd ed), Sage Publications, London

Rollison, Derek with Broadfield, Aysen (2002) *Organisational Behav-*

iour and Analysis: An integrated approach, Pearson Education Limited, Harlow

Smedley, Tim (2010) Gore tells HR: 'focus on long term' *People Management*, 15 July 2010

Essay 5

RESOURCING AND TALENT PLANNING

Aims of Essay 5
By the end of this essay, readers should be able to
- explain the importance of managing an appropriate balance of resources to meet the short and long term aspirations of organisational strategy;
- prepare plans to attract and retain key people with the capability to achieve that strategy;
- articulate ways of responding to the changing environment in which the public sector is operating.

Introduction

Employee resourcing is the collective term for a range of HR activities that follow the career of an employee from beginning to end in an organisation. These activities include recruitment and selection, the orientation of new employees and their deployment throughout their career, succession planning, absence control and turnover, and issues relating to release, redundancy and retirement. Over the past few years, the term *talent management* has joined the vocabulary of this aspect of HR, stressing the need for organisations to focus their recruitment and selection on candidates who are most likely to offer a long term commitment to the organisation in a manner that most effectively helps achieve its strategic objectives. The obligation on the organisation is to provide relevant opportunities for personal development to justify the appointment decisions made.

Thus, *resourcing and talent planning* covers a broad portfolio of activities which are aimed at ensuring that the organisation has a balance of people, in terms of numbers, skills and experience, to enable it to achieve as smoothly as possible the longer term aspirations of its strategy. Such a broad range of activities cannot be covered in detail in a short essay, so the aim of this present work is to offer brief insights into some of the current thinking on aspects of resourcing and talent planning and to identify case studies that illustrate good practice on an international basis.

Cultural considerations

It is important to note that there are strong traditions and cultural considerations in relation to resourcing in the public sector, between countries and even between parts of the sector in some countries. For example, it is general practice in some countries to recruit new entrants direct from school or university as generalists, following competitive examination or selection. Successful candidates might expect permanent employment, potentially a *job for life*. Career progression within the same organisation may be based on further competitive examination, as is the norm under Public Service Law in Japanese national and local government (Jichi Sogo, 1995:25–30, Smart, 2009, Kimura, 2010, CLAIR, 2010:27–29), or on performance and other relevant factors, as is generally the case in the UK national civil service.

By contrast, in the UK local government appointments tend to be to a specific vacancy or position following public advertisement and competitive selection. The appointment is to the specific authority. This arrangement is based on joint agreements between local government employers and trade unions dating back to about 1950. It is claimed to open selection up to the widest possible range of candidates and to encourage greater equal opportunities and diversity in employment. The implication for employees is that often they must seek career advancement by applying for positions with other local authorities, because career paths are closed to them if external candidates are appointed to what would otherwise be a promoted position for them.

It is appreciated that traditions and legislation might override the ability fully to transfer aspects of best practice between cultures: but it might be possible to adapt them.

Relating resourcing to other aspects of HR
No aspect of resourcing and talent planning can be undertaken in isolation from other parts of the HR function; they are all inter-dependent on one another. Thus, recruitment and selection must have attention to the structure of the organisation and to internal and external labour markets. Decisions on deployment or redeployment of staff, on promotion and job rotation, will impact on the *learning and talent development* functions (see Essay 6). And any decision that involves a reduction in the number of employees also implies the need for employee consultation and engagement (Essay 8), to ensure the plan is achieved with the least disruption to the organisation.

The developing emphasis on *talent management*
The thesis on which talent management is based is that all organisations need individuals with high potential to make a difference to their performance. They need the ability to identify, attract, develop and retain individuals who are of particular value to them, either in view of their 'high potential' for the future or because they are fulfilling business-critical roles. In other words, talent management is an holistic approach to HR, which seeks the best people to do the jobs critical to the achievement of objectives and then nurtures them along their career path. The process does not stop on the day the employee starts work for the organisation. Further information on this topic may be found on the CIPD Factsheet on Talent Management – see References at end of Essay.

According to an international survey *The Future of HR in Europe: Key challenges through 2015* undertaken by the Boston Consulting Group (2007:17) for the European Association for Personnel Management, talent management was ranked by both HR and other executives as the most important future topic at which they would like to excel, but also as the HR activity that executives said their organisations had the lowest capabilities in. The survey was, admittedly, focused on business leaders, but HR trends in business one day tend to become hot topics in the public sector the next. The report (BCG, 2007:7) suggests that the starting point for any organisation is an assessment of the number of employees with the desired education, experience and competencies it needs in the light of its strategic and operational requirements (see also Workforce Planning, Essay 3). From this assessment, the organisation should identify the specific types of employees they seek and the best avenues for reaching them.

Then, to retain high potential employees, organisations need to tailor career tracks so that they reward and fully utilise different types of employees with different interests and skill levels, and ensure that they build the loyalty of the employee to the organisation. BCG (2007:8) adds that attracting and retaining talent demands that organisations offer potential and current employees a value proposition that aligns closely with the desires of the employee as well as with the employer's brand (see also Essay 8, *Employee Engagement*).

Talent management as the holistic approach envisaged here is much more difficult to apply in those parts of the public sector where recruitment tends to be to specific vacancies rather than to a longer-term career. It could be argued that the basis of talent management already exists in those organisations where candidates are initially appointed as generalists, whose careers are developed over time. However, there are no doubt improvements that could be made to ensure that there is greater specificity in the way that *high potential* recruits are distinguished, in their continuous assessment, in their in-service development and in such issues as succession planning.

Since the concept of talent management is relatively new to the public sector, a summary of materials that might assist an organisation considering its introduction is listed in the references section. BCG report (2007:18) that respondents to their survey suggested appropriate actions as part of talent management might include developing tailored career tracks and specific compensation schemes for high potential employees, and targeting potential candidates by ethnicity or gender to create a more diverse labour force.

Attracting talent
Ward (2010) offers a five stage model leading to the appointment of new talent: *attract, source, assess, hire and on-board*. The first challenge is to attract interest from suitable candidates. The media used for announcing a vacancy or recruitment competition are critical. For positions that draw on the local labour market, the organisation's own website and newspapers are frequently the preferred sources of publicity (see, for example, IPMA-HR, 2006:4), along with local media. For more senior positions, where recruitment may be national, national media, employment agencies and executive search consultants may be used. In the UK, the Society of Local Authority Chief Executives (SOLACE, 2010a) offers its own consultancy support that works with public sector bodies in the attraction and recruitment of senior managers.

Discriminating applicants will conduct their own research about a potential employing organisation, using the internet and media to assess such issues as its reputation as an employer, its political structure and its record for financial prudence, before they decide whether to submit an application. In the UK, The Sunday Times annually conducts a series of surveys of the best employers to work for, including a survey specific to the public sector which lists the 75 best public agencies to work for, based on a survey of 45,000 employees of the 200 public bodies who sought to be included in the list. Such data may be persuasive in deciding whether to apply for a senior job with an organisation.

Assessing talent

The assessment process may be split between such predominantly bureaucratic tasks as administering personality, intelligence and aptitude tests and equal opportunities records, and checking such things as references and criminal records (IPMA-HR, 2006:30) and the more interpersonal aspects, particularly interviewing and assessment centre activities (SOLACE, 2010:9). Increasingly, public sector employers are adopting this more penetrating style of assessment for more senior appointments, which include such features as management exercises designed to test the ability of candidates to respond to the pressures of senior management, psychometric testing, one-to-one discussions between candidates and senior managers and politicians from the organisation, and an informal social event.

A carefully developed assessment centre should offer a number of benefits to any organisation seeking to improve its selection process, including better person-job fit and early identification of potential high-fliers. But to be effective, the tools of assessment must be carefully matched to the job in question and be validated against the types of candidates expected to apply. For example, the organisation should ensure that any psychometric tests used have been validated for all the cultural group(s) from which candidates might be attracted. Figure 5.1 offers a schematic for a strategy to enhance talent management in the public sector, based on that used by a multi-national corporation as reported by BCG (2007:19).

Assessment centres are not generally used for more basic level employees, although interviews may be complemented by aptitude and manual dexterity tests for machine operators and candidates for technical positions.

Welcoming new talent

The so-called *onboarding* stage of Ward's model refers to the new employee joining the organisation. Suffice it in this essay to reinforce

Short-term gains	Improvements	Longer-term initiatives
Identify talent needs and perform initial gap analysis (numbers needed - numbers in post)	Improve internal talent review • identify all high potentials in organisation • differentiate between review of performance and review of potential • consider a fast-track programme for high potentials • develop retention plan	Consider new initiatives: • key performance indicators for high potentials • specific development programmes • coaching and mentoring, job rotation
Target recruitment campaigns at preferred sources of candidates		Activate new talent pools •diversity programmes
Create an entry-level programme (recruitment, orientation, initial deployment and performance monitoring)		
Identify and build relationships with potential new talent pools		Provide active career management programme • agree potential career paths with individuals
Identify organisational implications – for HR, line managers, individual employees			
Create any new support systems – data bases, information flows			

Figure 5.1
Enhancing talent management in the public sector
(adapted from Boston Consulting Group (2007:19), with kind permission)

the importance of orientation (induction) to this stage, to obtain effective output from the employee in the shortest possible time; to reduce the likelihood of the employee from leaving quickly; and to enable the employee to develop a relationship with management and colleagues.

Retaining talent

Capelli (2000:103–111) observes perhaps somewhat controversially *that the old goal of HR management – to minimise overall employee turnover – needs to be replaced by a new goal: to influence who leaves and when.* All employee turnover has a cost, although where it is relatively easy to find and train new employees quickly and at relatively little cost, it is possible to sustain high quality levels of service provision despite having a high turnover rate.

On the other hand, the loss of key talent is potentially disruptive to the achievement of organisational goals, the smooth management of part or all of the organisation, and a loss of any investment made in personal development, relocation, special compensation package and so on.

Bevan *et al* (1997) suggest a risk analysis to quantify the seriousness of losing key people, or of key posts becoming vacant. Such an analysis includes identifying key people who may leave; estimating the likelihood of this happening and how serious the effects of a loss would be on the organisation; and assessing the ease with which a replacement could be found and the costs not just of appointing a successor, but also any consequential costs of development and compensation package. By contrast, Allen (2008:10), in an extensive review of retention, proposes strategies for what he calls *embedding* employees in the organisation and continues by illustrating how to develop a retention management plan.

There is evidence that during the recent economic downturn, turnover reduced as employees feared for their jobs and were unsure as to whether they would gain security of employment elsewhere. However, key employees with experience of successfully leading an organisation through a challenging period will always be in demand and therefore a plan should be in place to try to ensure that they do not leave for a better job in another organisation. Further information is also available in the CIPD Factsheet on Employee turnover and retention – see References.

Succession planning

Succession planning is about identifying the right people capable of filling vacancies as they arise and of filling potential gaps in the organisation. These might be employees who are seen as ready to fill a gap in the short term, or they may be those for whom some form of development, coaching or mentoring programme is deemed appropriate as part of a longer-term plan.

Succession planning has risen up the HR agenda on a more or less universal basis as public sector organisations appreciate the significant numbers of *baby boomers* due to retire over the next few years, especially amongst those who hold key senior management appointments (IPMA-HR, 2008; Improvement Service, 2008). Their retirement is one aspect of employee turnover that can be forecast, and should therefore be one focus of succession planning. As potential replacements for future retirees are identified, so it will become clearer for which other positions succession planning may also be necessary. Interestingly, perhaps, BCG (2007:21) reports that executives in Europe agree that they have not devised strategies fully to combat the demographic problem facing them, and rated their capability in *managing demographics* lower than all topics other than *managing talent*. Even at a time when the public sector in many countries is facing reductions in labour force as a consequence of budget cuts, it should be clear that succession planning should be a key HR activity.

Equalities and diversity

The relative focus on issues of equal opportunities and diversity in employment will vary between cultures and will also depend on the degree to which the public sector is working in a multi-ethnic, multi-national labour market. Thus, for example, the UK, USA and The Netherlands have well-developed codes relating to equal opportunities in employment irrespective of gender, race, religious affiliation, disability, age and sexual orientation. By contrast, some countries are more mono-cultural or drawn from a single ethnic group, and others for religious reasons would not include some provisions that are commonplace in the USA or the UK, where the diverse labour market potentially opens new talent pools.

Release, resignation, retirement and redundancy

The release, resignation, retirement and redundancy of employees are also part of the portfolio of activities that makes up *employee resourcing*. Their impact on the operational requirements of an organisation needs to be factored in to strategic workforce planning and to more routine HR activities, such as recruitment, succession planning and organisation redesign. It is difficult to forecast with certainty the level, nature and timing of voluntary resignations from an organisation, or the number of compulsory releases, such as dismissals on the grounds of misconduct, although most organisations will have historic data and trends on which they could build some form of estimates for planning and budgetary purposes.

The level of forthcoming retirements, on the other hand, will be relatively easy to estimate where an organisation has an agreed retirement age. A scan of personnel records will identify those employees who might be expected to retire – normally at the date of reaching a specified age. However, some countries, including the UK, are abandoning what is called the *default retirement age*: the age at which an employee must retire, unless their employer's pension provisions permit an element of flexibility. The removal of the default age reflects a political recognition that a large number of experienced workers will be lost to the economy unless they are encouraged to continue beyond the previously fixed retirement age, as well as the pragmatic recognition that many people remain fit beyond their early-mid 60s and therefore wish to decide for themselves the age at which they will retire. There is also a financial imperative that pensions' costs will be reduced, or at least will not increase at the previously prevailing rate.

Traditional retirement practices may no longer be fit for purpose since losing the valuable skills and expertise is the last thing that an organisation wishes to do. The scale of the problem being faced by many organisations is epitomised by the IPMA-HR report (2008), that within the US Internal Revenue Service, by 2013 35% of managers and 73% of executives will be eligible to retire, and that it is important for the Service to identify possible successors before the vacancies occur.

The final dimension to this essay on *resourcing and talent management* is redundancy. Many public agencies across the world are currently facing reductions in employment costs and staff numbers, with the prospect that some employees may have to be laid off, either on the basis of voluntary severance or on a compulsory basis. The processes by which redundancy decisions are made will be guided by national legislation, agreements with trade unions and local conventions. However, it is good practice to avoid as far as possible compulsory lay-offs, following the kind of redeployment and redundancy procedure summarised in Figure 5.2.

Cuts in public expenditure and in staffing levels are normally opposed by trade unions and employees. They may lead to industrial action, strikes and public demonstrations as they have in Greece, Spain and France. They frequently have to be implemented by local public agencies on the basis of primary decisions taken by national government. They certainly need sensitive handling, and the kind of process in Figure 5.2 should help to minimise the levels of compulsory action that tend to aggravate employee relations more than voluntary actions.

Concluding remarks
This essay has concentrated on aspects of *resourcing and talent planning* that ought to be of relevance to public sector organisations across many countries. It has sought to promote developments in

Stage 1	Assess current staffing levels and future staffing requirements by department/function and by staff group/type/profession
	Quantify excesses of current staff over future requirements
Stage 2	Model possible solutions • anticipated voluntary retirements • scope for relocation/redeployment/retraining of current employees • cost cutting opportunities, short of staff reductions (including freeze on recruitment, pay freeze or pay reductions, reductions in other staff on-costs, cuts in other parts of HR budget, cuts in non-staff budgets)
Stage 3	Open consultation with employees/trade unions/any other groups required by national legislation or local custom • discuss options • seek suggestions • seek agreement to options identified by management
Stage 4	Seek volunteers for voluntary retirement, voluntary relocation/redeployment/retraining, voluntary severance
Stage 5	Implement voluntary actions
	Review outcomes against stage 2 and redefine models of possible solutions
	Continue consultation
Stage 6	Implementation of compulsory actions as a last resort

Figure 5.2
Outline redeployment and redundancy procedure
© 2010 Dr Peter Smart

HR that relate talent management to the achievement of organisational objectives, that interlock with other aspects of HR and that reflect the challenging environment within which the public sector is operating. The references have been identified to illustrate the focus of the essay and to provide readers with access to far more material than space here allows.

References

Allen, David G (2008) *Retaining talent: a guide to analysing and managing employee turnover*, SHRM Foundation, Alexandria VA, at http://

www.shrm.org/about/foundation/research/Documents/Retaining%20Talent-%20Final.pdf

Armstrong, Michael (2001) *A Handbook of Human Resource Management Practice*, 8th edition, Kogan Page, London

Ashridge Consulting, part of Ashridge Business School (UK), at http://www.ashridge.org.uk/Website/Content.nsf/wCON/Talent+management?opendocument for general information and links on talent management

Bevan, S, Barber, I and Robinson, D (1997) *Keeping the best: a practical guide to retaining key employees*, Institute for Employment Studies, Brighton

Boston Consulting Group/European Association for Personnel Management (2007) *The future of HR in Europe: Key challenges through 2015*, Boston Consulting Group, Boston MA

Capelli, P (2000) A market-driven approach to retaining talent, *Harvard Business Review*, January-February, pp.103–11

Chartered Institute of Personnel and Development (2009) *Succession planning* (fact sheet), CIPD, London, at http://www.cipd.co.uk/subjects/hrpract/general/successplan.htm

Chartered Institute of Personnel and Development (2010) *Talent management: an overview* (fact sheet), CIPD, London, at http://www.cipd.co.uk/subjects/recruitment/general/talent-management.htm

Chartered Institute of Personnel and Development (2010) *Employee turnover and retention* (fact sheet), CIPD, London, at http://www.cipd.co.uk/subjects/hrpract/turnover/empturnretent.htm?IsSrchRes=1

Council of Local Authorities for International Relations (Japan) (2010) *Local Government in Japan*, CLAIR, Tokyo

Department for Work and Pensions (UK) (2010) *Retirement Practic-*

es: Making the right choice. An employer's guide, DWP, London Crown Copyright

Improvement Service (2008) *Managing Staff Training and Development*, Improvement Service, Broxburn, at http://www.improvementservice.org.uk/component/option,com_is_search/lang,en/?query=succession+planning&option=com_is_search&Itemid=986

International Public Management Association for Human Resources (2006) *2006 Recruitment and selection benchmarking*, IPMA-HR, Alexandria VA, at http://www.ipma-hr.org/sites/default/files/pdf/BestPractices/final5.pdf

International Public Management Association for Human Resources (2008) *Leadership Succession Planning in the Internal Revenue Service*, IPMA-HR, Alexandria VA, at http://www.ipma-hr.org/sites/default/files/pdf/BestPractices/LeadershipIRS.pdf

Jichi Sogo Centre (1995) *Local Public Service Personnel System in Japan*, Jichi Sogo Centre, Tokyo

Kimura, Seiki (2010) 'Comparing human resource management in Japan and the UK', *Myriad Leaves*, March 2010, Japan Local Government Centre, London

SHL (2010) *Assessment Centres*, at http://www.shl.com/WhatWeDo/Pages/AssessmentServices.aspx#assessment_centres

Smart, Peter (2009) 'Comparing local government employment practices: The UK and Japan' *Journal of the Japan Intercultural Academy of Municipalities*, July 2009, JIAM, Shiga-ken (published in Japanese)

Society for Human Resource Management (USA) at http://www.shrm.org/searchcenter/Pages/Results.aspx?k=talent%20management, includes helpful links to a range of publications on talent management

Society of Local Authority Chief Executives (UK) (2010), Assistance with recruitment of senior managers, at http://www.solaceenterprises.

com/factsheets/22042009/Recruitment%20&%20Selection.pdf

UK Local Government Improvement and Development (2010), at http://www.idea.gov.uk/idk/core/page.do?pageId=5222245, includes public-sector specific materials on talent management

Ward, Karen (2010) 'Talent management in recession and resurgence', *Converse*, the journal of Ashridge Consulting, Ashridge Business School, UK, accessed on-line at http://www.ashridge.org.uk/Website/Content.nsf/FileLibrary/9B09C8CD1AA9A3C7802577590039897D/$file/Talent%20Mgmt.pdf

Essay 6

LEARNING AND TALENT DEVELOPMENT

Aims of Essay 6
By the end of this essay, readers should be able to
- explain why learning is an essential ingredient for organisational survival;
- demonstrate the developmental and financial benefits of linking learning activities to the organisation's strategic objectives;
- argue why expenditure on talent development is a priority even in times of financial restraint.

Introduction

The focus of this essay is *learning and talent development*. The term *learning* is used in preference to the more traditional terms *education*, *training* and *development*, to stress the active part that employees must play in the process of developing their competencies and knowledge, as well as the responsibility of the employer to make learning opportunities available. The theme *talent development* builds on that of Essay 5 (*Resourcing and talent planning*), here emphasising the relationship between learning and development and organisational strategy.

The aim of learning and talent development is to ensure that people at all levels of the organisation possess and develop the skills, knowledge and experiences to fulfil the short and longer term ambitions of the organisation, and that they are motivated to learn, grow and perform. The learning may be as a result of traditional course-based training and education activities, or coaching and mentoring, or through self-directed, work-based process leading to increased adaptive capacity. The outcome of the process could be new knowledge or the development of a new competence, or changes in an employee's behaviour. The specific reference to *talent development* relates to the imperative that organisations nurture their high potential employees and other key members of staff, who are able to make a substantial contribution to organisation objectives, either immediately or in the longer term.

The essay also identifies some practical advice on how public agencies might seek to prioritise demands on limited development budgets to maximise the return on their investment. In any period of financial restraint, staff development budgets are often amongst the first to be cut, and frequently by a greater percentage than other staff–related costs. As Fujishima (2010) observes in a discussion on public expenditure decisions, *there is a tendency with projects such as personnel development to put them in the category of 'muda'* (Japanese, literally *waste* or *pointless*) *without enough debate of their role before cutting them*. There may be little chance that officials will be able to persuade the political decision makers that development budgets should be left intact, even though there is evidence from the private sector that this might be advisable (see, for example, Churchard, 2010a). The challenge for HR and line managers is to maximise the benefits of whatever budget is available.

Learning, talent development and organisational survival

There is evidence from a number of countries (including the USA, UK, Sweden, New Zealand and Japan) that the shape of the public sector is changing more rapidly than at any time in the past. New organisational structures, political accountabilities and business models require new ways of delivering services, almost certainly with reduced staffing levels.

Earlier evidence of this trend is available from the late 1980s/early 1990s onwards, as various aspects of the public sector were exposed to competitive tendering and as *Reinventing Government* (Osborne and Gaebler, 1992) and *New Public Management* became part of the lexicon of public sector management. But the impact of those developments will probably fade into insignificance compared with the changes in organisational structures, political management and staffing levels now being considered. For example, Suffolk County Council (UK) decided in September 2010 radically to change the way it provides services, from direct delivery to commissioning a wide range of its services and supporting other organisations to deliver them, in an attempt to reduce costs, reduce its size, and to cut out waste and bureaucracy (Suffolk County Council, 2010). The implication of such changes is that the staff who are left will require new competencies, leadership skills and flexibility in the range of tasks they are able to undertake.

Whilst the challenge of *organisational survival* has primarily been one for the private sector, commentators suggest that publicly-funded organisations are likely to be subject to greater competitive and financial rigour, and even to losing the right to deliver services if they fail to meet pre-determined standards. The corollary is that standards will be easier to maintain and improve if public agencies allocate their scarce development budgets following a careful process of needs assessment and prioritisation against their strategic and operational objectives. As public agencies recruit to replace staff reaching retirement age, so they will also need to develop the new talent to ensure the survivability of their organisation.

These points are emphasised by John Philpott, chief economist at the CIPD, who observes that politicians may not have fully considered the *enormous management challenge* that substantial cuts in public expenditure will have, creating a workforce that will be increasingly demoralised. Philpott concludes that *to get the best from (a demoralised) workforce will require a step change in management capability in the public sector* (Churchard, 2010b). Dean Shoesmith, president of the UK Public Sector People Managers' Association, concurs that whilst there are some capable leaders in the public sector, *there's a big piece of leadership and organisational development work to be done in most public sector organisations*, including skills in commercial acumen and leadership capabilities. (Churchard, 2010b).

The Catch-22, it seems, is for the public sector to find the money it needs to develop the talent it requires for future leadership and to deliver the services the public expect, whilst making the levels of financial savings that political leaders demand.

Relating talent development to organisational objectives
Every learning and development experience should relate specifically to the achievement in some way of the organisation's overall objectives. This may be to meet a short-term need, such as briefing employees in the requirements of a new piece of legislation that the organisation must implement, or it may have a longer-term purpose, to equip a high potential employee with leadership skills for future deployment.

Bird (2010) identifies three priorities for learning and development: to understand and ensure compliance, to focus on core skills and to gain competitive advantage. Compliance programmes may relate to legislative responsibilities (for example, health and safety training); to external requirements, such as continuing professional development to enable an employee to continue to practise in their profession (as might apply to a medical practitioner, a lawyer or a teacher); and to policy decisions internal to the organisation. Core skills are those essential for the smooth operation of the organisation, such as learning a new ICT system. In the public sector, *learning for competitive advantage* might at first sight appear a less relevant reason for employee development. Substitute the words *learning for greater organisational effectiveness* or *learning to deliver cost-effective services* and the reason for development becomes clearer, particularly if it can be shown that such learning opportunities are the drivers of long-term organisational goals.

In times of financial restraint, to achieve learning and development in each of these three areas is potentially more than some organisations might achieve. The aim should be to ensure that any expenditure on learning and development is based on appropriately assessed organisational priorities, adds value to the organisation and can be justified on financial and developmental grounds.

Showing a return on investment

It is important to evaluate learning and development at several levels. One is inevitably the perceived benefit of any learning experience to the recipient in terms of what has been learned and how effective the learning experience was. But as Bird (2010) argues, from the organisation's perspective, evaluation must be about calculating return on investment and the relative cost effectiveness of the various learning and development programmes provided or sponsored. In this way, the organisation will be better placed to explain why it has decided to continue to support some programmes, to discontinue some, and to find more cost effective ways of delivering others.

Talent development

Not all talent development and leadership training needs to be based on expensive classroom-based learning: there are innovative and less costly ways of providing learning experiences, including internal programmes, mentoring and coaching. Harrison (2009:103) cites a case study from Birmingham City Council (UK) which included visits to other organisations, work shadowing and mentoring. Each participant had to set their own goals for learning and then find largely work-based ways of meeting them. Participants learned skills of influencing, managing change, working in teams and thinking strategically. East (2010) explains how Oxfordshire Council (UK) implemented a career coaching scheme that helped staff better to understand what motivates them in their careers, to review their transferable strengths and to be aware of options for career and personal development.

Academic programmes, such as the MBA and MPA, offer a high quality learning experience connected with a postgraduate qualification. They have the advantage of learning with a high degree of academic rigour and the opportunity to synthesise outcomes to case studies drawn from the real world. In many countries, however, this is an expensive option, although in a few postgraduate education is offered at low, or even nil, cost.

Variety of international provision
There are many different approaches to talent development, between nations and also between different parts of the public sector in the same nation. For example, Japanese local public service law places local authorities under an obligation to provide training to officers to demonstrate or improve their efficiency (Jichi Sogo, 1995). In the UK and the USA, there is no similar general statutory provision, although the protective services (police, fire and rescue) have well-established training programmes for new recruits, for promotion purposes and for technical and leadership training.

The institutional structure for the delivery of development programmes also varies considerably. In the UK, there are training colleges for the civil service (http://www.nationalschool.gov.uk), for the police services in England and Wales (http://www.npia.police.uk) and in Scotland (http://www.tulliallan.police.uk) and for the fire service (http://www.thefiresafetyconsultancy.co.uk), but there has never been a comparable institute for local government. However, Local Government Improvement and Development (http://www.idea.gov.uk), the Improvement Service (http://www.improvementservice.org.uk) and the local government associations have links with providers of talent development. In addition, many local authorities have training centres of their own, as well as commissioning development programmes from external providers and sponsoring staff to attend academic programmes at universities and colleges.

Similar staff colleges for the police service exist in countries as diverse as Bangladesh (http://www.psc.gov.bd), Chile (http://www.escuelacarabineros.cl/) and Nigeria (http://www.policestaffcollege.com), and for the national civil service in many equally diverse countries, including Ethiopia (http://www.ecsc.edu.et), Singapore (http://www.cscollege.gov.sg) and India (http://www.asci.org.in). Similar institutions exist for local government in some countries, including Denmark (Local Government Training and Development, Denmark, http://cok.dk) and Japan (the Japan Intercultural Academy of Municipalities, http://www.jiam.jp). In Japan, every major local authority also has its own internal staff development centre offering a range of programmes for its own staff and for the staff of neighbouring smaller authorities. Individual states in the USA take different approaches, one example of which is the Alaska State Department of Personnel and Labour Relations *TrainAlaska* (http://aws.state.ak.us/TrainAlaska), as highlighted by the IPMA-HR (2010) (http://www.ipma-hr.org/hr-resources/hr-solutions/hr-solution-topics/training-programs). Sweden, on the other hand, used to have two national training centres, for municipalities and county councils, but they now run on a commercial basis and not just for local government employees.

Support for talent development in emerging democracies and developing economies is provided by a wide range of organisations, such as the Finnish Consulting Group (http://www.fcginternational.fi) and its Swedish partner, SIPU International (http://www/sipuinternational.se), which started life in 1979 as a government agency, the Swedish Institute for Public Administration, and was privatised into its present form in 1992.

As Kimura (2010) and Smart (2009) highlight in their respective comparisons of HR in local government in Japan and the UK, culture and traditions play a major role in the different ways in which talent development is undertaken in different countries, but this does not preclude consideration of other ways of doing things, by comparing current practices between countries.

Concluding remarks

In a short essay, it is impossible to acknowledge the full range of learning and talent development activities that are undertaken in the public sector and the benefits that inevitably accrue from them. The focus has therefore deliberately been on some of the hot topics that are confronting public agencies across the world, particularly in relation to budget constraints and the constant search for greater value for money. In this particular essay the opportunity has also been taken to provide links to a range of websites that will enable readers to assess for themselves the different approaches that exist in relation to learning and development.

References

Bird, Hedda (2010) 'How to calculate the return on L&D' *People Management*, 3 June 2010

Churchard, Claire (2010) 'Recovery puts focus on talent strategies' *People Management*, 6 May 2010

Churchard, Claire (2010) 'Leadership challenge as budget cuts bite' *People Management*, 1 July 2010

CIPD (2009) *Aligning learning to the needs of the organisation*, Fact sheet, CIPD, London, at http://www.cipd.co.uk/subjects/lrnanddev/general/alignlearng.htm?IsSrchRes=1

CIPD (2010) CIPD HR profession map, CIPD, London, at http://www.cipd.co.uk/hr-profession-map/explore-the-map.htm

East, Sam (2010) 'Developing a respected internal career coaching scheme for Oxfordshire council' *People Management*, 1 July 2010

Fujishima, Noboru (2010) 'The Director's Eye' *Japan Local Government Centre Newsletter*, September 2010, JLGC, London, at http://www.jlgc.org.uk/en/enewsseptember5.html

Harrison, Rosemary (2009) *Learning and Development*, 5th edition, CIPD, London

International Public Management Association – Human Resources (2010) *HR Solution Topics – Training Programmes* at http://www.ipma-hr.org/hr-resources/hr-solutions/hr-solution-topics/training-programs

Jichi Sogo Centre (1995) *Local public service personnel system in Japan*, Jichi Sogo Centre, Tokyo

Kimura, Seiki (2010) 'Comparing human resource management in Japan and the UK', *Myriad Leaves*, March 2010, Japan Local Government Centre, London

Osborne, David and Gaebler, Ted (1992) *Reinventing Government*, Addison Wesley, Reading MA

Smart, Peter (2009) 'Comparing local government employment practices: The UK and Japan' *Journal of the Japan Intercultural Academy of Municipalities*, July 2009, JIAM, Shiga-ken (printed in Japanese)

Suffolk County Council (2010) *Council services to be delivered differently in the future*, Suffolk County Council news release, 23 September 2010 at http://www.suffolk.gov.uk/News/NewsArchive/2010September/CouncilServicesToBeDeliveredDifferently.htm

Essay 7

PERFORMANCE AND REWARD

Aims of Essay 7
By the end of this essay, readers should be able to
> - articulate why public sector organisations need to build and reward a high performance culture based on critical skills, capabilities, experience and performance;
> - assess how their reward systems might respond to a high performance culture and also be equitable, market-based and cost effective;
> - propose ways in which their current reward system(s) might be developed to meet the organisational needs of the future.

Introduction
The continuing demand for financial restraint in the public sector has put employee reward under the spotlight. Public sector pay in many countries has come under attack from parts of the media, from members of the public, from the owners of small businesses and from many politicians. On the other hand, there is a view that myths and half truths abound, that there are too many public servants, who are overpaid and under-worked, and that it is difficult to measure and manage performance in the public sector.

Governments in various parts of Europe have intimated their intention to freeze public sector pay, or even to reduce it, leading to strikes and threats of industrial action. In the UK, there is an increasingly prevalent view that no public servant should earn more than the Prime Minister (although those who espouse this view seem to overlook the pay of senior managers in a range of quasi-commercial public sector organisations, such as the BBC and Royal Mail, and focus their attention almost entirely on senior civil servants and local government officials). In the USA some government agencies have been close to defaulting on payment of their employees during 2009–2010.

Whether or not the reader subscribes to any of the populist views is, it is suggested, irrelevant. There are several good reasons why it is time for public sector reward to be put under the spotlight. Pay systems have become generally inflexible, frequently relying on incremental progression which rewards length of service rather than effort or performance. They are based heavily on fixed rather than variable costs. Many systems can be traced back to the 1950s or earlier. In the UK the basis of many current public sector pay systems have their roots in nationally negotiated agreements initially concluded in the late 1940s (Kelly, 1992), even though there have been attempts to make them more market responsive in recent years. Public sector pay systems in the USA (Fox, undated) and in Japan (Jichi Sogo, 1995) have similar histories and structures, with a complex range of relatively inflexible incremental scales. In some countries, the public sector has tended to promote itself as a *good employer*, setting wage rates for lower paid employees above the nationally determined minimum wage. Whilst there may be good social arguments for this, there are also disadvantages at times of fiscal restraint.

Many public sector pay systems are, it is proposed, no longer fit for purpose and so need a thorough overhaul for the twenty first century. A number of approaches have been tried and others are currently under discussion. Some simplify the pay structure into job families with limited numbers of grades (Fox, undated), some propose to link pay to performance, others focus on aspects of total reward. The remainder of this essay will examine a number of these developments, and assess how some of them seek to relate reward to performance measures based on personal and organisational objectives.

Criteria for effective reward management
Shields (2007:34) notes that the primary objectives of any reward system are *to attract the right people at the right time for the right jobs, tasks or roles; to retain the best people by recognising and rewarding their contribution; and to motivate employees to contribute to the best of their capability*. Shields (2007:35) adds that a reward system should also be of value to employees in fulfilling their human needs; be equitable, or felt-fair, by offering rewards commensurate with contribution; comply with relevant legal requirements; and be affordable, cost-effective and aligned with the organisation's corporate objectives.

Anthony *et al* (1999:408) add that management must decide the importance of external equity in the organisation's compensation system and how closely compensation will be linked to the organisation's overall strategic plan, and choose between merit pay rises (paying for performance) and across-the-board rises. They also identify pay level policy, pay structure policy and the types of rewards offered as critical decisions in developing a pay system (Anthony *et al* (1999:414). (ANTHONY, *HUMAN RESOURCE MANAGEMENT 3E, 3E.* © 1999 South-Western, a part of Cengage Learning, Inc. Reproduced by permission, www.cengage.com/permissions).

There is an increasing focus on *total remuneration* and *total reward*. Many people think only of the financial rewards that make up total remuneration (base pay, variable pay such as bonuses or performance related pay, and benefits that have a financial value, such as holidays and sickness pay). They overlook the non-financial rewards (opportunity to develop skills, career opportunities and the quality of working life) that, taken with total remuneration add up to total reward.

Challenges of public sector reward systems
Critics of current public sector pay arrangements frequently overlook the diversity of the public sector, and the number of different

pay practices that have built up over time to reflect that diversity. In a health service, there may be different pay and benefits schemes for medical consultants, junior doctors, nursing staff, managerial and administrative staff, technicians and laboratory staff. In local government (depending on the services provided in different jurisdictions), there may be different schemes for managerial and administrative staff, technicians, teachers, craft and manual workers, police officers and fire fighters.

These different pay and benefits schemes may be applied locally by the employer on an autocratic basis, or they may be negotiated nationally between representatives of the employing authorities and trade unions representing employees. Agreements may be given legal effect, or there may be discretion as to whether they are applied by individual employers. There is the added challenge that in most countries, employees in the public sector may constitute up to 25% or more of the working population and therefore the force of numbers makes it difficult to make short term changes to long-standing agreements.

National legislation can impact as an external constraint on pay arrangements. For example, in the UK, equal pay legislation has required the public sector to find ways of ensuring that work of equal value between different groups of employee is recognised by equal pay. Finally, there exists a view that there should be a multiplier that would restrict the pay of the most senior employees in public agencies to not more than 'n' times that of the lowest paid. In the UK, discussions on this point suggest a multiplier ('n') of perhaps 20 times.

Responding to the challenges
A number of different responses, as illustrated below, have been discerned to the challenges posed.

Broad banding and job families

Broad banding replaces the traditional complex structure of narrow salary bands that have been a feature of public sector pay for so long, with a few wide bands. It reflects the trend in organisation design to adopt flatter structures, which requires fewer salary grades, which reflect the trend towards flatter organisations requiring employees with a more flexible range of competencies. The emphasis of broad banding shifts from job grade assignment to broad work roles (often called job families) and career development in those roles. Individual employees are placed within the range, depending on the competencies and contribution they bring to the job.

Competency-based career banding

Fox (undated) explains one specific public sector application of broad banding principles that was adopted by the state of North Carolina (USA) to streamline its 50 year old pay system, by adopting a competency-based career banding scheme. There are ten job families, each characterised by three competency levels requiring the demonstration of knowledge, skills and abilities from *contributing* (basic) to advanced. The scheme reduces the previous larger number of grades into more generic, wider pay ranges and allows pay movement based on the development and demonstration of competencies required for the position. The scheme, it is claimed, is an integrated competency-based HR system which links compensation with competency, performance management, recruitment and workforce planning.

Single status

Local government in the UK sought to implement the *equal pay for work of equal value* legislation by adopting what was called a *single status agreement* for employees previously covered by the national negotiating machinery for administrative, professional and technical staff and for manual workers. Previously, the administrative, professional and technical staff had been graded on traditional incremental scales which paid an annual salary according to the jobs they did, whilst manual workers had been paid an hourly rate, without incremental progression, according to the jobs they did, following an earlier job evaluation review.

The initial single status agreement was reached in 1997. The intention was to create a single *spinal column* of salary points, onto which all employees covered by the two former sets of negotiations would be assimilated, following a further job evaluation review to be conducted locally.

Whilst it was hailed as innovative, in seeking to bring so many local government employees within one scheme for pay and benefits, it has still not been fully implemented, with local authorities citing a range of reasons, including the costs of outcome on the pay bill and the costs of implementation (which has been estimated as millions of British pounds in many authorities), union expectations and problems with the job evaluation scheme (Local Government Employers (LGE), 2004, LGE, 2006 and UNISON, undated a, b). The agreement has also raised new tensions between groups of employees: for example, those engaged in traditionally male occupations, who were historically paid more for *heavy labour* are aggrieved because those in occupations predominated by females have been regraded upwards to reflect skills such as caring for vulnerable children and adults. The implementation of the single status agreement also offered the opportunity at local level to incorporate some form of broad banding, but evidence from the Local Government Employers (LGE, 2006) indicates a continuing preference for narrow banded salary scales.

The growing focus on relating pay and performance
It could be argued that many manual employees in the public sector have had their pay related to performance for many years through so-called productivity bonus schemes. The best were based on objective measurement and a variable element of pay was awarded for

above standard performance (that is, the performance that might be expected of the average employee asserting average effort to do the task allocated). On the other hand, very little attempt had been made until relatively recently to find ways objectively of measuring the performance of managerial, professional and administrative staff and to award them some element of variable pay based on either personal, group or organisational performance.

As Cooke (2010) explained at a conference on public sector pay in the UK (autumn 2010), the adoption of performance measures and performance related pay in the public sector requires the right leadership capability and continued cultural transformation which permits performance issues and organisational behaviours to be tackled. At the same conference, Kennerley (2010) noted that the record of the public sector to create an effective link between pay and performance by defining success and linking it to pay is typically poor.

What is *performance*?

There are many definitions of *performance*, but the common emphasis tends to be on linking what individual employees, or teams of employees, do, to achieve the strategic objectives of the organisation. It is about how things are done as well as what is done. Shields (2007:21) illustrates an *open system model* of performance, comprising three elements on a linear sequence: *inputs*, including employee knowledge, skills and competencies; human resource *throughputs*, the activities that transform inputs into outcomes including work effort and behaviour; and *outputs*, including the outcomes from work behaviour – see Figure 7.1.

Why and how should performance be managed?

Armstrong and Barron (2000:7) define *performance management* as *a strategic and integrated approach to delivering sustained success to organisations by improving the performance of the people who work in them and by developing the capabilities of teams and individual con-*

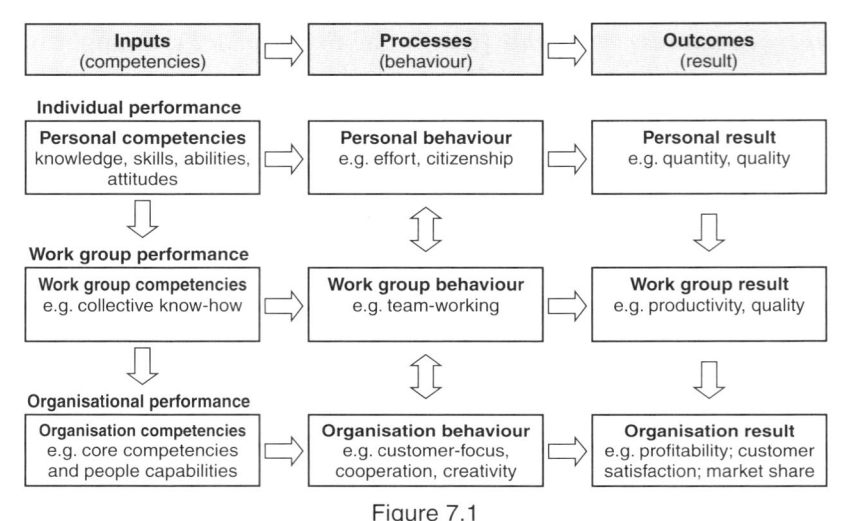

Figure 7.1
The interlocking dimensions of performance

Inputs (competencies) → Processes (behaviour) → Outcomes (result)

Individual performance
- Personal competencies: knowledge, skills, abilities, attitudes
- Personal behaviour: e.g. effort, citizenship
- Personal result: e.g. quantity, quality

Work group performance
- Work group competencies: e.g. collective know-how
- Work group behaviour: e.g. team-working
- Work group result: e.g. productivity, quality

Organisational performance
- Organisation competencies: e.g. core competencies and people capabilities
- Organisation behaviour: e.g. customer-focus, cooperation, creativity
- Organisation result: e.g. profitability; customer satisfaction; market share

(Shields, John, 2007, *Managing Employee Performance and Reward: Concepts, Practices, Strategies*. © John Shields 2007, published by Cambridge University Press, reproduced with permission)

tributors. These include providing clarity about who is accountable for ensuring objectives are achieved, with whom, by when and what the expected outcomes are; focusing the organisation on priorities; providing a balanced approach to evaluating performance; and allowing feedback to individuals and teams.

Ideally, the process should start with the highest level strategic objectives of the organisation, which are then cascaded down to successively lower levels in the organisation, identifying who does what to ensure the strategic objectives are achieved. In theory, if it is not possible to identify such lower level objectives for an individual or team, it could be argued that they have no contribution to make to the organisation.

The basis of performance management is the *performance management* cycle. Shields (2007:23) offers a six stage performance management cycle: *action planning, learning and development, monitoring, informal feedback, formal assessment or rating, diagnosis and formal review, relating at each stage to three performance criteria of competencies, behaviour and results and goals.* There are many different systems of performance management, often based on what are called *SMART Objectives*, that is, *specific, measurable, achievable, realistic, time-bound.* Any system should naturally be tailored to the specific needs of the organisation to ensure that it is fit for purpose.

Rashid (1999) has a UK perspective. Popovich (1998) takes the concept of performance management further, from a USA perspective, in developing a thesis of *high-performance organisations* in the public sector. These are defined as *groups of employees who produce desired goods or services at higher quality with the same or fewer resources. Their productivity and quality improve continuously, (...) leading to the achievement of their mission* (Popovich, 1998:11). He adduces a number of reasons for his approach, including fiscal pressures, voter demands for better performance and the growing number of people in government who are determined to encourage employees to improve productivity and quality in whatever they do.

Rewarding performance
Shields (2007:352–353) identifies a number of reasons for the introduction of performance-related reward: increasing employee motivation, altering performance standards, increasing labour cost flexibility and transforming employee values, attitudes and behaviour to elicit higher levels of organisational commitment and organisational citizenship behaviour. There are clearly benefits of introducing performance-related rewards in the public sector, but Anthony *et al* (1999:421) identify a number of potential problems with pay for performance schemes. These include quantifying and defining performance standards against which variable rewards may be assessed; the mind-set and culture of the organisation and the people within it; who decides the level of performance-related rewards; and the po-

tential demotivating factors of performance-related decisions. For a scheme to be effective, its aims have to be clearly specified, and it has to be carefully designed and properly communicated to gain buy-in at all levels, realistic and affordable and monitored as it is applied. The choice and design of a scheme is for the individual organisation to decide, taking account of the best advice available.

Additional resources
Each of the publications cited in this essay contains examples of performance management schemes in the public sector, which may be accessed for further research. Additional resources include the following. The CIPD has factsheets giving general advice on pay structures (http://www.cipd.co.uk/subjects/pay/general/pay-structures.htm), and on performance management (http://www.cipd.co.uk/onlineinfodocuments/atozresources.htm and http://www.cipd.co.uk/NR/rdonlyres/AC5B3F1D-CA83-4CB2-AD97-9B2333411133/0/Performance_management_in_action.pdf). The IPMA-HR has a number of examples of best practice in public sector pay for performance (http://www.ipma-hr.org/hr-resources/successful-practices/list-topics/Compensation). The UK Local Government Employers have items on pay systems (http://www.lge.gov.uk/lge/core/page.do?pageId=119825), broad banding (http://www.lge.gov.uk/lge/core/page.do?pageId=119821 and performance related pay (http://www.lge.gov.uk/lge/core/page.do?pageId=119829). The Swedish Association for Local and Regional Authorities has a booklet (SALAR, 2010) which includes a summary of current pay developments in Swedish local government, including national and local determination of pay, including the introduction of *individual pay*.

Concluding remarks
There is much more that could be written about *performance and reward*. For example, little or nothing has been said about benefits other than pay or about public sector pensions. Nor has there been space to illustrate the sections on performance management and per-

formance related pay with practical examples. However, it is hoped that the penultimate section, with information about a range of additional resources, will offset some of these shortcomings. It is clear from the amount of time and space being allocated by the media to public sector pay and pensions issues, certainly within Europe and the USA, that these are topics that have caught the imagination of the public and politicians – and much of the coverage has irritated public servants and their trade unions. They are therefore issues on which politicians, HR practitioners and line managers need to have an understanding, and to be able to respond when they are challenged, whether politically or professionally as to *what they intend to do about public sector pay.*

References

Anthony, William P, Perrewé, Pamela L, and Kacmar, K Michele (1999), *Human Resource Management: A strategic approach* 3rd edition, The Dryden Press, Fort Worth

Armstrong, Michael and Barron, Angela (2000) *Performance management: the new realities*, CIPD, London

CIPD (2010) *Factsheet on pay structures*, at http://www.cipd.co.uk/subjects/pay/general/pay-structures.htm

CIPD (2010) *Factsheets on performance management*, at http://www.cipd.co.uk/onlineinfodocuments/atozresources.htm and http://www.cipd.co.uk/NR/rdonlyres/AC5B3F1D-CA83-4CB2-AD97-9-B2333411133/0/Performance_management_in_action.pdf

Cooke, Mike (2010) *Reward in the public sector*, Director of Organisation Development and Deputy Chief Executive, London Borough of Camden, speaking at a CIPD Forum, 29 September 2010

Fox, James C (undated) Career-banding – A Competency Based Human Resources Classification and Compensation System, Fox Lawson and Company, St Paul MN at http://www.ipma-hr.org/sites/default/files/pdf/BestPractices/bp_CBJimFox.pdf

IPMA-HR (2010) *Best practice information on pay for performance*, at http://www.ipma-hr.org/hr-resources/successful-practices/list-topics/Compensation

Jichi Sogo (1995) *Local Public Service Personnel System in Japan*, Jichi Sogo Centre, Tokyo

Kelly, Geoff (1991) *A history of LACSAB: Industrial Relations in Local Government 1947–1991*, Centurion Press, London

Kennerley, Liz (2010) *Linking performance to reward*, Senior Reward Consultant, Hay Group, speaking at a CIPD Forum, 29 September 2010

Local Government Employers (2010) *Broad banding*, at http://www.lge.gov.uk/lge/core/page.do?pageId=119821

Local Government Employers (2010) *Pay systems*, at http://www.lge.gov.uk/lge/core/page.do?pageId=119825

Local Government Employers (2010) *Performance related pay*, at http://www.lge.gov.uk/lge/core/page.do?pageId=119829

Local Government Employers (2004) *Single status local pay reviews survey report - Autumn 2004* at http://www.lge.gov.uk/lge/aio/52809

Local Government Employers (2006) *LGE survey of pay structure development July 2006*, at http://www.lge.gov.uk/lge/aio/52812

Popovich, Mark G (1998) *Creating high-performance government organizations*, Jossey Bass, San Francisco

Rashid, Noorzaman (1999) *Managing performance in local government*, Kogan Page, London

Shields, John (2007) *Managing Employee Performance and Reward*, Cambridge University Press, Port Melbourne, Victoria, Australia

Swedish Association of Local and Regional Authorities (2010) *Employer perspectives on local authorities and county councils: facts and analysis 2010*, SALAR, Stockholm

UNISON (undated) *Single status pay and grading* at http://www.unison.org.uk/localgov/gettingequal/singlestatus.asp

UNISON (undated) *Equal pay now – funding for local government*, at http://www.unison.org.uk/localgov/gettingequal/

Essay 8

EMPLOYEE RELATIONS AND ENGAGEMENT

Aims of Essay 8
By the end of this essay, readers should be able to

- explain the need for the maintenance of good employee relations, for the benefit not just of the organisation and its employees, but also of the citizens the organisation serves;
- assess the impact when external forces, such as central government economic policy, interfere with the established relationship between a public sector organisation and its employees;
- identify practical ways in which the public sector can maximise on a mutually acceptable basis the efforts of its employees.

Introduction
This essay examines two main perspectives on the relationship between the organisation and its employees. First, it assesses the need for the relationship to be managed appropriately within a clear and transparent framework underpinned by organisation practices and policies and, ultimately, by relevant employment legislation. The aim must be to ensure as far as possible the continuity of service delivery to the citizens served by public agencies, without disruption from strikes and other forms of industrial action.

It is perhaps too simplistic to observe that citizens have a legitimate expectation that the services for which they pay, through taxes and other charges, will be provided without interruption. It is certainly easy to imagine the consequences of garbage not being collected, of caring services being withdrawn, of fire fighters declining to turn out in response to an emergency, and of air traffic controllers causing the suspension of flights. On the other hand, there might just be occasions when recourse to industrial action is appropriate as a last resort, when all of the procedural and legal arrangements for dispute resolution have been exhausted. The onus on employer, employees and trade unions alike is to ensure, as far as practicable, that the contingency does not arise.

Second, the essay investigates what has traditionally been described as *employee commitment* and is now increasingly called *employee engagement*. This implies not just that employees will discharge the strict legal requirements of their contracts of employment, but that the employer has in place processes that ensure that all aspects of the employment experience are positive and understood. As Boston Consulting Group (2007:41) observe, whilst the employer's workplace must provide an atmosphere that is focused on and driven by performance, employees need to be motivated so that they become emotionally engaged with the organisation.

The essay seeks to summarise some of the key arrangements that employers can make to ensure the achievement of its objectives and the continued delivery of service, through good employee relations and constructive employee engagement.

EMPLOYEE RELATIONS IN CONTEXT

It is difficult to propose a single universal model of employee relations, in view of the different legal frameworks and national and local cultures and traditions within which the relationship between employers and employees is set. However, there is a common basis for ensuring the maintenance of good relations between employers and employees, which Gennard and Judge (2002:9) summarise as *the continued achievement of the organisation's business and/or social objectives through the reconciliation of any differences between employers and their employees*. Management and employees share a common interest to resolve any differences between them, since a breakdown in their relationship could lead to actions such as strikes or work to rule that disrupt the smooth delivery of services to the customers of the organisation, and a consequential loss of pay for the employees who are taking disruptive action.

The two main *players* in any employment relationship are the individual employer and the individual employee, governed in legal terms by the contract of employment between them and in motivational terms by the *psychological contract* between them. The latter may be defined as *a set of reciprocal but unwritten expectations that exist between an individual employee and the organisation he or she works for* (adapted by present author from Armstrong, 2001:237).

In addition, depending on the national framework for employee relations, the employer may belong to the appropriate employers' organisation (in their respective jurisdictions, for example, the Local Government Employers in England and Wales (http://www.lge.gov.uk), the Convention of Scottish Local Authorities (http://www.cosla.gov.uk) and the Swedish Association of Local and Regional Authorities (http://english.skl.se/web/english.aspx)), and the employee may belong to a trade union or staff association. Many jurisdictions also have third party organisations who participate in employee relations, particularly at moments when arbitration or conciliation is required between parties to a dispute.

Furthermore, depending on local culture, traditions and legal code, there may be other mechanisms available to the players by which they agree rules to govern the employment relationship, to set procedures to settle local differences, and to enable the views of the respective parties to be sought on proposals and issues that might impact on employees. These mechanisms include local collective bargaining, consultation, communication processes, employee involvement and participation and procedures that relate to the hearing of disciplinary issues and grievances, and to discuss matters relating to health and safety.

Trends in employee relations in the public sector

There is a tradition going back some 60 years or more, particularly in the UK and northern Europe, for pay and the main conditions of employment of public sector employees to be determined by national negotiations between the employers' association(s) and the trade union(s) (Kelly, 1991). The outcome of such national collective bargaining has then been applied locally by the individual employing agencies as part of the legal contract of employment with individual employees.

However, over the past 25 years or so a number of changes have occurred. First, where national negotiations still exist, they have tended to provide more of a framework within which individual employers conclude local agreements with trade unions for local application (see references in Essay 7 on *single status* and *local pay*). Second, in the UK, the determination of pay and conditions of employment for a range of public sector employees has been withdrawn from collective bargaining and replaced by what are known as *pay review bodies*. These are independent of government, although they work within strict terms of reference laid down by government. They hear representations from employers and trade unions, and then decide the level of award to be made. They cover the Armed Forces, the National Health Service, teachers in England and Wales, the prison service and senior civil servants (Office of Manpower Economics, 2010). Third, there is a greater incidence of local collective bargaining replacing, or complementing, the traditional national structure, with some agencies seceding from the national arrangements altogether.

By contrast, as Anthony *et al* (1999:622) explain, the tradition in the USA is quite different. It was not until 1962 that President John F Kennedy granted certain groups of public workers the right to bargain collectively in all aspects of their jobs except wages, the right to which was subsequently granted in 1970.

There is also evidence of diminishing levels of trade union membership amongst public sector employees in some countries, a trend that is common to the private sector. However, as the CIPD point out (2010a:4), in the UK the proportion of public sector workers who are members of trade unions is now greater than in the private sector.

The impact of external influences
Perhaps the greatest challenge to employee relations in the public sector currently comes from the fairly universal tightening of fiscal policy, having a potentially adverse affect on services and jobs. During 2010 there have been an increasing number of strikes by union members in many countries across Europe, demonstrating against cuts in public expenditure and a freeze on increases in public sector pay, and against proposals to increase pension age.

The public sector is the one over which central governments have greatest financial control. Yet, the public sector in most countries is made up of hundreds, potentially thousands, of individual employers. The *public sector* is not generally one single employer. So, whereas the trade unions and their members are protesting against policies of central government, it is the relationship between individual agencies, who have no direct influence over central government, and their employees that is being disrupted. As the CIPD (2010a:3) observe, *the combination of reduced pay, jobs and pensions on a hitherto unprecedented scale seem likely to represent the 'perfect storm'*, potentially enabling trade union leaders to promote further action if they believe they have the support of members and public opinion. The test might be whether action taken by public sector employees against central government policies can occur without souring local employee relations, in both the short term and the longer term.

The employees of some public services, such as police officers, in some countries are forbidden by law from striking. In its discussion on employee relations in the public sector, the CIPD (2010a:7) observes that many essential services, such as electricity, gas and water supply, are now delivered by privatised companies and that any consideration to outlaw strikes would need to be extended beyond the public sector. They form the conclusion, which might be equally valid in other democracies, that making industrial action in essential services unlawful would probably carry a very high risk of confrontation and that enforcing such a law against *large numbers of angry public sector workers could present real problems of policing*.

In addition to fiscal and economic policy, central governments are also instrumental through national legislation in establishing the minimum standards of behaviour in various aspects of the employment relationship. Some laws are designed to protect the interests of the employer, such as legislation requiring a ballot of trade union members and the service of notice before industrial action is taken. Most, though, seek to protect the interests of employees against the actions of less scrupulous employers, in regard to such issues as health and safety, unfair dismissal and equal opportunities in employment. The challenge for HR and senior management is to ensure that they develop the appropriate policies and procedures, in consultation with trade unions as appropriate, to apply the requirements of the legislation.

Engaging employees in the workplace

Even at the most stable of times for employment, an organisation will want employees who will contribute willingly and effectively to the achievement of its objectives. At the same time, employees will prefer to work for an employer who encourages them to use all their skills and knowledge and permits them to use their initiative. When job security is under threat, as it is in the public sector in many parts of the world, employees may be uncertain about their futures and so may be less willing to put in extra effort. So, it is incumbent on the public sector to identify practical ways in which it can maximise on a mutually acceptable basis the efforts of its employees. This will require a process of *employee engagement.*

The term *employee engagement* has only entered the dictionary of HR during the past ten years and gained common usage in the past five. Before that, the comparable focus was on finding ways of gaining *employee commitment* and on creating opportunities for *employee involvement.* In current usage, employee engagement can be seen as a combination of commitment to the organisation and its values, and a willingness to help out colleagues (through what is increasingly referred to as organisational citizenship). Engagement goes beyond job satisfaction and is not simply motivation. It is something the employee has to offer: it cannot be required as part of the employment contract. It is internationally acknowledged that an engaged workforce consists of employees who will help their employer achieve organisational objectives by doing their best, because the employer is able to offer jobs that are worthwhile.

There are clearly resonances with the HR outcomes of *commitment* and *congruence* that form important elements of the Harvard Model (Beer *et al*, 1984), yet *engagement* is something more. There are also qualities drawn from a balanced psychological contract, which Sims (1994) observes, requires a *continuing, harmonious relationship between the employee and the organization.* Sims continues that a *violation of the psychological contract can signal to the participants that the parties no longer share (or never shared) a common set of values or goals.* The motivational theories of the behavioural scientists are also applicable.

The challenge is to create the right environment that enables the organisation and its employees to maintain the harmonious relationship that Sims refers to. This is a matter of discussing and agreeing these requirements with individuals and teams: two way communication is an important element of good employee relations. Schneider (2010) advises that jobs designed for engagement are those that capture the hearts and minds of workers, demand the full use of important skills and abilities, and are a challenge. They must be meaningful and provide for personal growth and development be designed to promote efficiency and allow for cooperation to get work done. It is management's job to ensure that employees are treated as stakeholders, relying on consensus and cooperation rather than control and coercion.

Engagement is not always easy
The CIPD research (2010a:3) suggests that the ingredients for building any real level of employee engagement in the UK public sector are currently absent. Employees feel let down by their senior managers who appear too frequently to be defending decisions taken by their political leaders; the levels of trust between management and employees are low compared with colleagues in the private sector; employees do not generally feel that they are consulted or treated with respect, nor do they have a clear sense of where the organisation is going (CIPD, 2009). If this is the situation in the UK, is it likely to be any better in France, Greece, Ireland, Spain or any of the other countries where national government policy appears to be a selective attack on the public sector? It could be argued that, with the options for budget cuts set before individual public agencies over recent times, they have no clearer sense of direction than the employees who work for them.

Yet the MacLeod Report (MacLeod and Clarke, 2009) is relatively buoyant about the impact that employee engagement can have on the success of organisations. They admit, though (MacLeod and Clarke, 2009:4) that it is hard to see how the quality of public service to which the population aspires can be achieved without putting the enthusiasm, commitment and knowledge of public services at the forefront of delivery strategies, especially since the services face the reality of an end to years of rapid growth in investment. They also note (2009:5) that within the public sector there is a growing understanding of the importance of engagement as a medium for driving the performance and well-being of public servants. They cite the decision of the UK Civil Service to carry out a service-wide survey of employee engagement for the first time, in 2009.

One conclusion that might be reached is that employee engagement will become ever more critical to the public sector, if the most dire of forecasts are proved to be correct, that the size of the public sector workforce will shrink. Clearly it is not a feature of employee engagement that workers should be expected to work harder for less pay, but a smaller, enthusiastic, motivated workforce, encouraged to work smarter in return for performance related rewards might actually be the kind of engaged workforce the public sector needs. This will, however, potentially challenge the mindset and culture of politicians, management and employees alike.

Concluding remarks

As with each of these essays, there is so much more than could be written, on topics such as employer branding (see for example CIPD, 2009b, 2010c, SHRM, undated) and *how to be a best employer in the public sector*. However, to conclude this overview of employee relations and employee engagement, the following suggestions from BCG (2007:42) are summarised. First, employee engagement is not purely an HR responsibility; rather, many of the primary activities lie in the hands of line managers, who must motivate their workforce and thereby improve organisational performance. Second, create emotional engagement in the workplace by developing empowerment and creating opportunities for personal growth; provide a supportive environment; and develop shared vision, values and pride.

References

Anthony, William P, Perrewé, Pamela L and Kacmar, K Michele (1999) *Human resource management: A strategic approach*, 3rd edition, The Dryden Press, Fort Worth

Armstrong, Michael (2001) *A handbook of human resource management practice*, 8th edition, Kogan Page, London

Beer, Michael, Spector, Bert, Lawrence, Paul R, Qinn Mills, D and Walton, Richard E (1984) *Managing Human Assets: The Groundbreaking Harvard Business School Program*. The Free Press, New York

Boston Consulting Group (2007) *The future of HR in Europe: Key challenges through 2015*, The Boston Consulting Group Inc/European Association for Personnel Management, Boston MA

Chartered Institute of Personnel and Development (2009) *Employee outlook survey 2009*, CIPD, London

Chartered Institute of Personnel and Development (2009) *Employer branding: maintaining momentum in the recession*, CIPD, London, at http://www.cipd.co.uk/subjects/corpstrtgy/empbrand/_employer_branding_in_a_recession.htm

Chartered Institute of Personnel and Development (2010) *Building productive public sector workplaces: Developing positive employee relations*, CIPD, London, at http://www.cipd.co.uk/publicpolicy/_employeerelations

Chartered Institute of Personnel and Development (2010) *Employee engagement: fact sheet*, CIPD, London, at http://www.cipd.co.uk/subjects/empreltns/general/empengmt.htm

Chartered Institute of Personnel and Development (2010) *Employer brand*, CIPD, London, at http://www.cipd.co.uk/subjects/corpstrtgy/empbrand/employerbrand.htm

Gennard, John and Judge, Graham (2002) *Employee relations*, 3rd edition, CIPD, London

Kelly, Geoff (1991) *A history of LACSAB: Industrial relations in local government 1947–1991*, Centurion Press, London

MacLeod, D and Clarke, N. (2009) *Engaging for success: enhancing performance through employee engagement*. Department for Business, Innovation and Skills, London, Crown Copyright, at http://www.bis.gov.uk/files/file52215.pdf

Office of Manpower Economics (2010) *Review Bodies* at http://www.ome.uk.com/Review_Bodies.aspx

Schneider, Benjamin (2010) *Engaged, but not always satisfied*, report on speech to SHRM's Special Expertise Panels, at http://www.shrm.org/hrdisciplines/employeerelations/articles/Pages/NotAlwaysSatisfied.aspx

Sims, R R (1994) 'Human resource management's role in clarifying the new psychological contract, *Human Resource Management*, 33(3), Fall, pp.373–82

Society for Human Resource Management, undated *Employer branding and retention strategies*, SHRM, Alexandria VA, PowerPoint® and Instructors' notes at http://www.shrm.org/Education/hreducation/Pages/BrandingandRetentionStrategies.aspx

Introduction to Part 3

Part 3 consists of two essays. The first is a fairly extensive reflection on the management and leadership of the HR function in the public sector. It includes an assessment of ways in which the HR function can imaginatively and proactively seek to influence the success of the public sector, against the financial and other constraints under which it is likely to be working for a number of years. It also investigates some of the ways that the HR function itself might be resourced: what the appropriate talent is, where it might be recruited from and how it might be developed.

There is also a brief reflection on the information needs of the HR function in the 21st century, to help make it fit for purpose.

Then the final essay in the book attempts, somewhat briefly, to assess the kinds of transformations that the HR function might be required to undergo, and how it might develop the capacities to help other senior managers continue to achieve their own objectives. This last chapter will never be the last word, simply a snap shot in time, since no one can forecast what new challenges the world will face over the next few years.

Essay 9

LEADING AND MANAGING THE HUMAN RESOURCES FUNCTION

Aims of Essay 9
By the end of this essay, readers should be able to
- identify the criteria that ensure the HR function is fit for purpose;
- assess the capabilities and organisation design that will ensure the HR function adds value to the organisation.

Introduction
It could be quite easy to become pessimistic about the future of the HR function. Reports in the HR press can appear both critical and unsupportive.

Tiplady, cited in *People Management* (2010a:12), warned an HR forum in the UK in summer 2010 that public sector HR needed to become more cost-effective if it was to survive the threat of being *priced out as an expensive overhead*, although he added more positively that the current economic situation was in fact an opportunity for HR to make an impact and take centre stage. The challenge for HR practitioners is to ensure somehow that they can confidently make the transition from perceived on-cost to a strategically focused ally of the rest of the organisation (more of this in Essay 10).

Also in the UK, the CIPD has launched a campaign to dispel *negative perceptions of HR as a career*. Graduates, it seems, perceive HR to be an unexciting bureaucratic profession, best to be avoided. The campaign publication stresses that the profession is increasingly focused on long-term organisational success (CIPD, 2010a). It cites the need for organisations to recruit people who will, individually and collectively, stay with an organisation and perform to the best of their abilities, and quotes recent surveys in *The Economist* and *Harvard Business Review* that both rated talent as a top three priority for executive boards. It promotes HR as a stimulating, interesting and challenging career offering personal and professional rewards.

In the USA, Calo, writing in *HR News* (2010a:10), noted that while HR claims it offers great potential to the organisation, it is the function within organisations that *most consistently under-delivers*.

To gain credibility, as well as to make a more positive contribution to their organisations, HR must become more strategically focused. There also seems to be a case for more positive promotion of the function as a career opportunity. So what can HR in the public sector do to prove that it is fit for purpose and capable of adding value, in these turbulent times, and is an attractive place to work?

Measuring fitness for purpose and added value
There is no magic formula to ensure that HR is fit for purpose and able to offer added value to the organisation, although there are a number of actions that an organisation might take to help HR overcome the kinds of criticisms that have been expressed.

The first is to determine what purpose the HR function is to serve within the organisation. Is the function to retain the reactive, operational characteristics of the traditional personnel function? Or is it to be encouraged to adopt the proactive, strategic nature of HRM (Holbeche, 2009, see Essay 2, Figure 2.1)? Is it going to deal solely with internal issues, or is it going to be responsive to the stimuli and challenges of the external environment (Beer *et al*, 1984)? Which of the various roles identified by Buyens and de Vos (1999, see Essay 2, Figure 2.6) will HR play, or where in the four bands of professional competence of the CIPD's HR Profession Map (CIPD, 2010b, see Essay 2, Figure 2.7) will it sit?

Conventional wisdom suggests that the HR function in most organisations will be a blend of proactive and administrative, strategic and operational. However, if the pundits are to be believed (and there appears no reason why they should not), the focus of HR will increasingly be on the contribution it can, and should, make to the achievement of overall organisational objectives and less on the traditional bureaucratic functions. After all, it appears that much of the criticism of HR as being an expensive overhead and ineffective service deliverer is pointed at the more traditional aspects of the function. In many organisations, HR still needs to make what Ulrich and Beatty (2001:293–307) described as the *move beyond its polite (people focused) and police (regulation focused) roles and add value to executing an organisation's strategy*. Public sector HR practitioners and line managers need look no further than successive editions of *People Management* (UK), *HR News* (USA) and similar publications in their own countries to see how often this message is highlighted.

In this connection, Boston Consulting Group (BCG, 2007:9) observe that to gain the trust of other senior executives, HR must get the fundamentals of their function right by *mastering HR processes* and by *transforming HR into a strategic partner*. HR must increase efficiency and effectiveness by systematically assessing and improving all its basic processes. This might include, for example, outsourcing support services or relocating them to shared service centres. To be a strategic business partner, HR must be able to *demonstrate business acumen, pragmatism and efficiency, whilst supporting cultural change and increasing overall skill levels in the organisation*. To prove that the HR function is adding value to the organisation, it must be able to measure its performance against qualitative, quantitative and financial metrics.

Wain (2010:17) comments that the HR person who is *perceived as justifying their own function, budget and very existence will engender far less trust than the one who appears to have the end goals of the or-*

ganisation uppermost in all that they do. The function needs to focus on the value that effective HR creates for the organisation, concentrating on outputs and outcomes, rather than on inputs. Moreover, it needs to focus on what the organisation values.

Models of service delivery

It is possible to trace a series of step changes in the way in which HR has been delivered within organisations over the past 30 or 40 years, being the time period over which the function has generally developed in the public sector world wide. The models summarised in the following paragraphs relate predominantly to those countries, such as the UK and the USA, where HR is seen as a coherent approach to people management within the organisation, and where HRM is seen as a profession in and of itself. Of necessity the historical development of the various models has to be generalised. They may not apply in the same way in countries such as Japan, where HR is not a discrete profession in the same way, and where the same coherent approach to people management may not culturally and traditionally have prevailed.

Central HR function

The starting point in many public sector organisations was the traditional central personnel department. Initially, this will have undertaken a range of predominantly control functions, in terms of monitoring and approving employee numbers and pay and grading issues. Its advisory role in relation to employment legislation became more prominent in many jurisdictions as the legal code was expanded to cover basic employment rights, employee relations, and equality, diversity and discrimination issues, from the mid-1970s onwards. Indeed, it is possibly in the record keeping and monitoring aspects of such issues as equalities that HR has gained most criticism for establishing what many line managers see as unjustified paper trails (whether this is a fair criticism or not is left to readers to decide). Another common criticism is whether, for example, a member of HR staff needs to attend selection interviews, where frequently it is the line manager of the appointing department who is accountable for decision making.

During the 1960s and 1970s, many central departments also set up staff development units and developed an expertise in health, safety and welfare. Some larger public agencies also permitted the appointment of HR staff in operational departments, which often appeared to duplicate some of the work of the central function.

Decentralisation of the HR function
In the 1980s and 1990s, there was a trend to decentralise some of the staff of the HR function to operational departments, with a staff relationship retained between the centre and the dispersed structure. It was during this period that there was limited evidence of outsourcing some of HR activities, particularly in the areas of staff development and specialist support in recruitment and selection.

The HR business partner model
The HR business partner model gained prominence from the early 1990s onwards. In this model of service delivery, the HR function appoints named practitioner(s) to be the main link between the centre and operational departments. As Ulrich and Beatty (2001:293-307) observe, for the transition to the business partner model to be truly effective, those engaged as HR partners need *to 1) know the business, 2) become an expert in HR basics (the function's 'tool kit') and 3) learn how to use these tools to change the organisation's culture and strategic capabilities through effective and efficient development of its workforce*. The extent to which the model has, in the public sector, truly reflected what Ulrich and Lake (1990) intended depends on the acceptance of the role of the HR partner and their own ability to demonstrate that they have the capacities required of an effective partner.

Moving from business partner to player

As part of their thesis, Ulrich and Beatty (2001:293-307) observed that HR professionals must always be *'becoming', constantly changing and adapting*. They argued that HR professionals need to move beyond partner to become players, *in the game, on the field, making a difference through their HR work*. In order to become players, they suggested, HR professionals had *to learn to coach, architect, build, facilitate, lead, and provide a conscience to business leaders*. It is for readers to decide whether the HR staff in their organisation have these capabilities, and therefore fully to be a player alongside senior management in the service delivery departments.

Developing a greater strategic focus

In 2009 Ulrich *et al* reiterated the view that the *biggest challenge for HR professionals is to help their respective organisations succeed* (Ulrich *et al*, 2009:6). In government agencies, they said, this may mean helping the rest of the organisation deliver services, achieve externally imposed goals, meet constituent needs and operate within reduced budgets. Their thesis was that too often HR focuses internally on the function of HR rather than externally on what customers need HR to deliver. They concluded that transforming HR professionals into business partners is not an end in itself, but the means to a strategic, business-oriented end.

Factors inhibiting a strategic focus in the public sector

Truss (2009:717–737) acknowledges the influence of writers such as Ulrich on the development of HR, but notes that HR has had a particular difficulty in establishing a strategic foothold in the UK public sector. She identifies a number of factors that may serve to constrain HR's role, including *the multiplicity of stakeholders, the strength of central government imperatives, targets and control mechanisms, and legacy factors concerning HR's traditional role*.

Against Truss's somewhat downbeat assessment, Ulrich still believes that HR is capable of leading the way in making organisations more sustainable in the wake of the economic crisis (Brockett, 2010:11). He observes that *HR people should see themselves as a professional services group within their own organisation, (whose) job is to assess the resources available and use their knowledge to determine how best to transfer those resources to client productivity.*

Ulrich does, however, add that recessionary pressures often induce the wrong response in HR and organisational leaders. Leaders can, he says, *go back to command and control*, to what they are familiar with, with the consequence that *HR risks going back to concentrating on transactional processes and cost-cutting*. Using a metaphor, he advises that in a downturn you will have to prune the tree, but don't cut out the root system.

Shared services organisations

The latest model of HR service delivery is the shared services department or organisation. The trend began in the late 1990s, when public agencies merged the leadership of the HR function with that of other central support services, such as policy development, finance, ICT or legal services. The aim at the time was to save costs by reducing the number of departments and delayering management structures.

In the past year or two, the trend has been to merge the HR functions (and other so-called *back office* activities such as ICT and finance) of two or more public agencies as a further means of cutting overheads. For example, the IPMA-HR's *HR Bulletin* of 29 October – 5 November 2010 reports the establishment of the Regional Training and Development Consortium for Public Agencies, a collaboration of cities in San Mateo County, California, USA. The purpose of the consortium is to provide training and development programmes, management tools and resources to public sector agencies in a way that will increase efficiencies and reduce costs, while sustaining the quality and variety of programmes available to public sector employees (IPMA-HR, 2010).

In the UK, there are several organisations that are successfully delivering shared HR services to two or more local authorities, particularly in the London area. However, as the final draft of this essay was being prepared, media reports suggested that this is a trend that is gathering momentum in the UK, with clusters of up to eight public agencies in discussion about sharing service delivery in front line services as well as support services such as HR.

Commissioning external provision of HR support
There is also evidence that public service organisations are proposing to commission the external provision of potentially the complete range of HR services as part of a wider political decision to outsource as many of their services as possible to commercial organisations and third sector bodies.

Is there one right model of service delivery?
The conclusions that Truss (2009:717–737) reached no doubt reflect the reality of HR in at least that part of the UK public sector that she reviewed. There are almost certainly some public agencies that have advanced little beyond the delivery of a traditional personnel function. On the other hand, there are clearly other agencies that are more strategically focused and in which the model of service delivery is more closely aligned to the business partner model or the shared services model.

Brockett (2010:11) concludes that Ulrich's message echoes that of the CIPD's Next Generation HR research project and their corresponding Shaping the Future project, which is introduced into the discussion in Essay 10. These projects are seeking to determine how HR is likely to change in future years and to determine the drivers of sustainable performance and the barriers to change.

As with so many of the issues covered by the present publication, the conclusion has to be reached that there is no right or wrong model. Whilst from the conceptual or theoretical point of view there may be strong arguments for a particular approach, there are so many forces at play in the public sector that organisations will move forward at different speeds towards what is perceived as a model of best fit.

A new approach to HR?

HR sometimes only has itself to blame for its reputation as a self-serving growth industry, an expensive bureaucracy, and the creator of unloved policies and procedures. Certainly, the body of employment legislation in many countries, including the UK and the Scandinavian nations, has for 40 years or more required employers to introduce disciplinary and grievance procedures, health and safety committees, consultation on proposed redundancies, and many other items. In the USA there have been similar legislative pressures, particularly in relation to diversity and equal opportunities. HR departments have devised their own internal record-keeping on such issues, in case an aggrieved employee or job applicant seeks redress for perceived unfair treatment under relevant legislation.

However valid some of these developments are, they are frequently perceived as an unwarranted on-cost by senior managers in other departments. In the UK public sector there is a continuing debate on the ratio of HR staff to total number of employees, with a view that 1:100 may be *about right*. The present author challenges the validity of this approach as too simplistic, failing to take account of outsourcing of HR work, the use of ICT for HR tasks, and the relative complexity of different public agencies. It is suggested that a more scientific assessment of various factors, including workload, contribution to organisation strategy, centralisation/decentralisation of HR and outsourcing/use of shared services, based on the principles of TQM and kaizen, is a more valid, although potentially more expensive, approach.

So is there some new approach that HR in the public sector could be taking? Essay 3 referred to the advice from former US vice-president Al Gore, that HR should focus on the long term (Smedley, 2010:14). CIPD chief executive, Jacqui Orme, believes the most important change that HR can make is to *demonstrate their competence in terms of knowledge (what they need to know), activities (what they need to do) and behaviours (how they will do it)* (MacLachlan, 2009:6). She also believes that public agencies are *crying out for the sort of strategic, principled contribution that HR leaders are already providing in the best organisations*, able to monitor short-term operational effectiveness and safeguard the longer-term health of the organisation. And gurus such as Ulrich, as we have already seen, are prolific in their outpourings of advice and profuse in their development of new or iterative approaches to HR.

Placing HR leaders under the spotlight
Any talk of a new approach to HR in the public sector puts the leaders of the function under the spotlight. They must be clear what the organisation is seeking to achieve and how their function can best support the development, implementation and monitoring of strategy. They must have a strong personal track record of operational excellence, political and leadership skills and vision. They must also have the capacity to coach and mentor the talent within their own function to contribute to the best of their ability. As Orme puts it, *only those HR leaders who have established their professional kudos will be able to rise to the opportunity* (MacLachlan, 2009:7).

The potential problem is that there may not be sufficient of these *paragons of HR professionalism* to go around. Depending on the size and structure of the public service, the scale of this potential problem will vary between countries. In the UK, the demand will be for several thousand practitioners at the most senior levels in the public sector. In Japan or the USA, with their larger populations and more complex structures of government, the requirement will be proportionately greater. Even at subordinate levels in the HR function, a problem may still exist. For example, concern has already been expressed in the UK that there will be a lack of negotiating skills in the National Health Service to support a shift from nationally to locally negotiated pay (Stevens, 2010:6).

Shoesmith (cited in Pickard, 2010:19) promotes the merger of the HR functions of two or more neighbouring public agencies into a *shared services* centre. This reduces the number of senior managerial staff and offers potentially substantial savings in salaries and other costs to the subscribing organisations.

In brief, to quote the CIPD (2010b), the most senior HR practitioners in the future should be able to *lead and manage a fit for purpose HR function*. They should have a *strong track record of operational excellence and a deep understanding of organisational requirements*.

Furthermore, they should be able to ensure that the function has *the right capability, capacity, and organisation design*, and that HR employees are *fully engaged, work collaboratively and possess a deep understanding of organisation and the drivers that create value*. This will require them to exercise team activity planning and execution, to ensure that the whole function is steered towards the common goal of delivering the service that the organisation needs. They will also need to understand and be responsible for the management of the HR budget.

Concluding remarks

It is difficult to write about the HR function in the public sector without appearing in some ways critical of how it has developed over the past 30–40 years. It is true that it began primarily as a monitoring and control function, with the aim of seeking to ensure equity of treatment and fairness in decisions made in relation to the employees of the public agency. This sense of fairness has commendably prevailed in established democracies, in the way in which most public agencies deal with their employees. Yet it is the attempt of the function to monitor the people-related activities of the agency that seems to have attracted much opprobrium in more recent times.

Over the same period, the function can claim many successes, in seeking to implement good employment practices, in ensuring that the public sector acts in an ethical manner, and in developing employees who are well qualified and competent to serve the tax paying public. Yet, critics might argue that good employment practices can be costly in terms of wages and related costs, and that this is one reason why competitive tendering and outsourcing, and an emphasis on *best value* had to be introduced in to the management of the public sector.

It is also true, as Truss (2009) records, that external forces have been responsible at times for holding back HR in the public sector from developing at the same speed and with the same emphasis on strategic HRM as in many organisations in the private sector. Yet, there are examples from many parts of the world that public agencies faced with the same external constraints have experimented with, and succeeded in, developing new forms of service delivery and in introducing practices of best fit that the private sector would be pleased to be associated with.

So much, it is suggested, depends on the professionals who head the HR function within public agencies, the encouragement that they receive from the political leadership and the senior management with whom they work. The final essay in this book will seek to address the qualities that are appropriate to leading the HR function in a visionary, strategic and proactive way.

References

Beer, Michael, Spector, Bert, Lawrence, Paul R, Qinn Mills, D and Walton, Richard E (1984) *Managing Human Assets: The Groundbreaking Harvard Business School Program*. New York, The Free Press

Boston Consulting Group (2007) *The future of HR in Europe: Key challenges through 2015*, Boston Consulting Group, Inc/European Association for Personnel Management, Boston MA

Brewster, Chris and Harris, Hilary (1997) *International HRM: contemporary issues in Europe*, Routledge, London

Brockett, James (2010) 'See HR as a professional services firm, says Ulrich', *People Management*, 25 March 2010, p11

Buyens, D and de Vos, A (1999) writing in *International HRM: Contemporary Issues in Europe*, eds Brewster C and Harris, H, London, Routledge

Calo, Thomas J (2010) 'Workforce and succession planning: no longer a zero-sum game', *HR News* (IPMA-HR), September 2010, pp.9–11

Chartered Institute of Personnel and Development (2010) *The truth about HR: the inside track on careers in human resources*, CIPD, London, at http://www.cipd.co.uk/NR/rdonlyres/D394EEAB-B886-4400-90AA-A539F226B12A/0/The_truth_about_HR.pdf

Chartered Institute of Personnel and Development (2010) *HRM Profession Map*, at www.cipd.co.uk/hr-profession-map

Holbeche, Linda (2009) *Aligning Human Resources and Business Strategy*, 2nd ed, Oxford, Butterworth-Heinemann

International Public Management Association – Human Resources (2010) *HR Bulletin*, IPMA-HR, Alexandria, VA at http://www.ipma-hr.org/publications/hr-bulletin/102910#5

MacLachlan, Rob (2010) 'A 'generational change' for the HR profession', *People Management*, 19 November 2009, p6

People Management (2010) 'HR must provide better value for money, warns Met's Tiplady' (editorial), *People Management*, 1 July 2010, p12

Pickard, Jane (2010) 'A cut above', *People Management*, 6 May 2010

Smedley, Tim (2010) 'Gore tells HR: 'Focus on long term', *People Management*, 15 July 2010, p14

Stevens, Michelle (2010) 'HR negotiating skills bar to NHS local pay', *People Management*, 29 July 2010

Truss, Catherine(2009) 'Changing HR functional forms in the UK public sector', *The International Journal of Human Resource Management*, 20: 4, 717–737

Ulrich, Dave, Allen, Justin, Brockbank, Wayne, Younger, Jon and Nyman, Mark (2009) *HR Transformation: Building human resources from the outside in*, McGraw Hill, New York

Ulrich, Dave and Beatty, Dick (2001) 'From partners to players: extending the HR playing field', *Human Resource Management*, Winter 2001, Vol 40, No 4, pp.293–307, © 2001 John Wiley and Sons, Inc

Ulrich, D and Lake, D (1990). *Organizational capability: Competing from the inside out*, Wiley, New York

Wain, Daniel (2010) 'Add value, not spin', *People Management*, 20 May 2010

Essay 10

HR IN THE PUBLIC SECTOR: THE NEXT STEPS?

Aims of Essay 10
By the end of this essay, readers should be able to

- assess the current expectations of and response to the HR function in the organisation with which they are connected;
- identify ways in which the function might become more strategic and add value to the organisation.

Introduction
Readers will have noted from earlier essays that the HR function in the public sector is not without its critics, particularly amongst senior managers in operational departments (for example, CIPD, 2010a, Calo, 2010, Wain, 2010). HR is felt to be too bureaucratic, too expensive and over-staffed. It is not seen as an agent for change. In some senses, it may not even be perceived as part of management, but as a function which is as keen to preserve the interests of the employees as it is to promote the interests of the employer. What is more, it is not universally seen as sufficiently capable of contributing to the development and implementation of overall organisational strategy.

Truss (2009) provided one explanation, that HR in the public sector is constrained by internal and external forces. Yet there is evidence from IPMA-HR and PPMA, for example, that the HR function is permitted and encouraged to take a leadership role in an increasing number of public agencies.

One confusing factor in this debate is the fact that there is no one common model of HR. Essay 2 reflected on the diverse range of activities that constitute the HR function, from administrative support to strategic leadership (Buyens and de Vos, 1999; CIPD, 2010b). Thus, it is feasible for an organisation to define the boundaries of the HR function as it sees it, perhaps based on the perceived capabilities of the practitioners in post, rather than from a more visionary point of view based on what the HR function is able to contribute to the leadership of the organisation.

The purpose of the final essay in this book is therefore to discern whether there are any tools that HR practitioners in the public sector can devise and use, to help the function add greater value, become more strategic and, at the same time, leaner and fitter for purpose.

Shaping the future and *next generation HRM*

Before that, though, it seems appropriate briefly to review two aspects of research underway in the UK to add to the references to the work of researchers such as Ulrich referred to in Essay 9 (Ulrich and Lake, 1990; Ulrich and Beatty, 2001; Ulrich *et al*, 2009). Both emanate from the CIPD.

Shaping the future

The first is the CIPD's *Shaping the future programme*, a longitudinal action research study exploring sustainable organisation performance. Its aim, states the CIPD, is to *advance thinking and practice through generating new insight, provoking debate, and providing practical guidance and tools that can be applied in a work context* (CIPD, 2010c).

The first interim report of the project (CIPD, 2010d) observes that *successful organisations sustain their performance over time, not just in the short term or through good economic periods. Indeed, the current unpredictable economic context has made the issue of sustainability even more crucial for organisations across all sectors.* The report identifies three drivers of sustainable performance: leadership, engagement and organisational development, as well as culture, communication and assessment and evaluation as further enablers of sustainability. The CIPD has conducted core research in six organisations, three of which (the BIG Lottery Fund, Birmingham City Council and NHS Dumfries and Galloway) are in the public sector, in view of the considerable changes facing that sector. The interim report develops the findings as case studies, with references to such HR related topics as flexible labour forces and the contribution of middle managers across the organisation to the organisation development programme. The report also has an extensive bibliography of related materials.

Next generation HR

The second piece of research is the CIPD's *Next generation HR* project (CIPD, 2010e), looking at the changing nature of HR and what the CIPD calls *some of the best and next emergent practice work that HR functions are engaged in*. The research, which has also involved a number of public sector respondents, is intended to stimulate debate about how HR will develop over the next five to ten years. The CIPD admits that it did not start this process from a neutral point of view but on the thesis that the crucial need is for HR not only to support short-term performance but also to put driving sustainable performance at the heart of its purpose. The implications of this, the CIPD concludes, are that HR needs to place much greater emphasis on building the foundations for future success and also play a much stronger role in holding the organisation to account for the unintended impact of decisions or behaviour on the long-term health of the organisation.

Future-proofing the organisation

The first report of this project floats a number of issues for further consideration. In order to *future-proof* the organisation, the HR function needs to be able to challenge what it is required to do, and to work with line managers and employees to build much greater levels of trust and *emotional loyalty*, ensuring that staff are treated in the same way as the organisation treats its customers. The function also needs to work on building an *agile culture* that is able to respond quickly to trends and opportunities (and, indeed to threats that might otherwise question the very survival of the organisation), and find ways of creating *future-fit leaders*.

The CIPD uses the concept of HR as *organisational guardians*, designing balanced HR policies and processes that support progressive ways of running the organisation, citing that the design of performance management, talent development and reward processes (amongst others) is an exceptionally powerful vehicle for taking organisations forward in particular ways. The research also proposed the concept of an *insight-driven approach to HR*, which demonstrates a deep understanding of what helps make an organisation successful – or stop it from being so – together with a deep appreciation of *what goes on around here* and *what really makes things happen here* based on its people, politics and culture. It expresses such organisational insight in terms of three qualities: *business savvy*, *organisational savvy* and *contextual savvy*.

The CIPD proposes that having an appreciation of these three factors enables HR to shape its activities in what it calls *five very powerful ways*. First, HR strategy becomes more responsive and relevant, with HR able to allocate resources and effort where they are needed in light of what is actually happening in the organisation on an ongoing basis. This, the CIPD observes, avoids the danger of HR being disconnected from the main activities of the organisation or too process heavy, rather than truly responsive to what is needed. Second, HR moves beyond being a service function towards establishing a proactive agenda, as it offers insight into things that others in the business may well not be seeing or acknowledging. This insight enables HR to establish its own agenda in a way that is joined up and relevant to the organisation, but not solely defined by the views of the current executive team or a current business plan.

Third, HR can act as an *early warning system* where the organisation is not alert enough to the changing demands placed on it. Fourth, it can provide insight into how to make the difficult things happen. Fifth, HR should be seen as an integral part of the organisation, where it would be inconceivable to think about driving strategy and activities forward without their involvement and perspective. In this way the unique expertise of HR is being applied to the real organisation-critical challenges in a timely and integrated way (adapted from CIPD, 2010e:15).

Next generation HR leaders

Two substantive questions arise from the research. First, what qualities will the new generation of HR leaders require? Second, where will HR be positioned in the organisation?

The first conclusion is that next generation HR leaders will be recognised by other senior leaders as having a real share in the voice and influence of the organisation. The second is that they will be able to demonstrate an *unusual ability to encourage new ways of doing business and identifying new areas of strategic focus*. They will have subtle and sophisticated skills of influencing people more senior in the hierarchy, the kind or organisational insight already referred to, and the ability to stimulate debate, influence opinion and use the dynamics of the organisation to advantage.

They will demonstrate such personal characteristics as a strong underlying sense of purpose, and such fundamental values as truth, respect and a lightness of touch and humility when dealing with assertive senior managers. They will explore ideas and stimulate debate patiently but with resolve, using the courage of their convictions to challenge prevailing wisdom when required. They will normally have a personal presence and natural authority that goes well beyond their official role in HR, confident in their own abilities yet not conflict averse.

Essay 9 has already observed that there may not be sufficient *paragons of HR professionalism* to go around. Add to professionalism the qualities identified by the CIPD for *next generation HR leaders*, and the availability of such talent may be even more restricted. Finding and recruiting such talent, or exploring ways to develop it from within existing resources, will be a major challenge for those public sector organisations that wish to establish themselves in the forefront of HR talent management and development.

The positioning of the HR function
The CIPD concludes that next generation leaders will bring quality and relevance to core HR responsibilities, whilst raising expectations of what HR can offer to support new ways of service delivery now and for the future, irrespective of whether they have membership of the senior management team or not since their wisdom and involvement will be both welcomed and demanded. From the public sector perspective, the positioning of the function depends largely on the expectation that the politicians, mayor or chief executive officer has of HR's actual or potential contribution to the organisation, especially where this is matched by an HR leader who is capable of offering more than the activities that have always been done.

The CIPD make the perceptive observation that senior leaders who have high expectations of HR and an instinctive feel for and belief in the importance of the people and cultural elements of organisation tend to be much more receptive to the expansive and dynamic agenda that an insight-rich, future-facing function can offer their organisation. On the other hand, those senior leaders who have a purely rational view of business will often end up with a much more limited and transactional HR function and this easily sets up negative spirals that undermine HR's potential value. Therefore, it could be said that every organisation gets the HR it deserves. So, where does HR sit in the organisation with which you are associated?

Tools for self-assessment
Several times in the book, the observation has been made that there is no right or wrong answer to the question *what role does HR play in your own organisation?* The influence of organisational culture and tradition, internal and external forces, the political perception of the role of HR, the strength of personality and professionalism of the HR leader and his/her staff and many other factors will determine its position within the organisation. The function is where it is and its current position cannot simply be changed.

If the function is already strategically oriented and the leader demonstrates some or all of the characteristics of a *next generation leader*, then it is amongst the minority of 20% of organisations that are *already there* (to quote Ulrich, cited by Brockett, 2010:11) in terms of building sustainability (and amongst an almost certainly even smaller minority of public sector organisations). If it is showing some movement towards such a positioning, then it is amongst the majority of 60% of organisations. But, Ulrich suggests, there is some 20% of organisations who will *never get it*. The remainder of this essay consists of a number of self-assessment tools, designed first to assist readers assess where the HR function in their own organisation sits against a number of models and ranges and second, to encourage them to assess some of their own capabilities and developmental needs, against criteria mentioned at various points in the book.

The assessment tools have been designed specifically for this book, based on the author's personal experience of leading an HR service in the public sector for nearly 20 years, taking account of the various observations set out elsewhere in this book. They are offered primarily for personal reflection and do not claim to have been validated by previous respondents.

Positioning the HR function

The first tool enables readers to assess how their function relates to the Buyens and de Vos (1999) model and the CIPD HR Profession Map.

Buyens and de Vos

On the following continuum, mark an X against each of the types of activity undertaken by your HR function. Then try to assess the percentage of time spent on each of the activities. Finally mark with a Y the area of activity on which, in your opinion, the organisation places greatest emphasis (see Essay 2 and Figures 2.2, 2.3 and 2.4 for definitions).

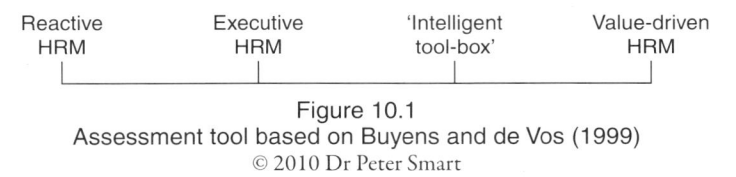

Reactive HRM	Executive HRM	'Intelligent tool-box'	Value-driven HRM

Figure 10.1
Assessment tool based on Buyens and de Vos (1999)
© 2010 Dr Peter Smart

CIPD HR Profession Map

Do the same against the four CIPD bands of professional activity (see Essay 2 and Figure 2.5)

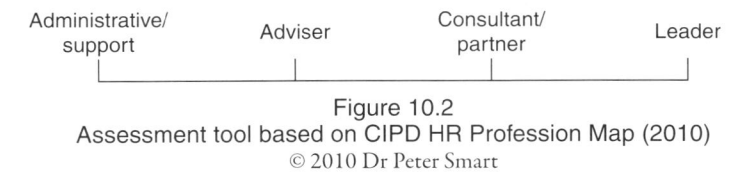

Administrative/ support	Adviser	Consultant/ partner	Leader

Figure 10.2
Assessment tool based on CIPD HR Profession Map (2010)
© 2010 Dr Peter Smart

Now, assess why you have answered as you have. Is the current positioning of HR historic, or has some conscious decision been taken in, say, the past year or two to re-position the function? If the latter applies, has it moved the predominant area(s) of activity to the right on the continuum (that is, emphasised the higher level areas of activity? Or has it moved it to a more reactive, passive service?

Lastly, using the same two figures, indicate the percentage of time you would prefer the service to allocate to each of the four areas of activity, and where you would personally prefer the predominance of time and effort to be spent.

Next, refer to Table 2.1 (Holbeche, 2009). Which of the two columns best reflects the approach taken to HR within your organisation? Does your answer to this exercise reflect the responses you have already given to the assessment tools based on Buyens and de Vos and CIPD HR Profession Map?

From these exercises, you should now be able to articulate the positioning of HR in your organisation. How does it compare with the views of writers such as Ulrich and his colleagues, in terms of positioning in line with current or recent thinking? Or has your organisation either failed to keep abreast of thinking, or chosen not to follow recent trends?

Is HR sensitive to its environment?
The Harvard Model (Beer *et al*, 1984) stressed the relationship between the HR function and the external and internal environments within which it is operating: *the situational factors* and the s*takeholder interests*. Review the Model against the extent to which the HR function in your own organisation relates to these situational and stakeholder factors. Try to rate the attention that is paid to each, and the ways in which they affect the development of organisational and HR strategy. Lastly, identify any situational factors or stakeholder interests that are not included in the Harvard Model, and conduct the same exercise with them.

Is HR strategic?
You will have started to address the extent to which HR in your or-

ganisation is strategic, when you assessed the function against Buyens and de Vos, and the CIPD HR Profession Map. Review your responses to that exercise and assess the ways in which the function could have a greater strategic focus. What, if anything, is holding the function back? What steps would you recommend to your political leaders or senior managers to increase the function's strategic influence?

Is the function close to being next generation?
First, assess how *insight-driven* you are. Do you see yourself as *business savvy, organisational savvy* and *contextual savvy*? If you are not the head of the HR function, make your own private assessment as to how insight-driven he or she is. Then, try to work out a personal development plan that would enable you to become more business, organisational and contextual savvy.

Next, look at what the CIPD calls the *five very powerful ways* in which HR can seek to shape its activities, by addressing the following questions.

To what extent is your organisation's HR strategy responsive and relevant? Is it able to allocate resources and effort where they are needed (in other words, have freedom of action), or is it constrained by political or managerial control?

Does HR have a proactive agenda, or is it seen as a service function? Does it have the capacity to offer insights into things that others in the business may not see or acknowledge?

Does it monitor the internal and external environments so that it can alert the organisation to changes before they impact directly on the people employed in the organisation? Does it, in military or secret service terms, have the intelligence function, to watch what is happening to labour markets, to salaries and conditions of employment offered by similar organisations, to assess the reaction of trade unions to possible changes in working practice, and so on?

Is HR seen as an integral part of the most senior decision-making bodies in the organisation? Does it have an input to all major strategic decisions, bringing a unique HR perspective? Is its advice applied by the decision makers?

The more you can answer 'yes' to these various questions, the closer your organisation is likely to be to *next generation HR*.

And, finally, you: are you a **next generation leader?**
These are potentially stressful questions to answer. Don't be too discouraged if you cannot say 'yes' to some or all of them. You will not be alone, by any means. The questions relate to developing thinking arising from some of the newest HR research that the writer is aware of.

First, are you recognised by politicians and other senior managers as having real voice and influence in the organisation? Is your advice listened to, respected and acted upon?

Are you able to demonstrate an ability to encourage new ways of doing business or identifying new areas of strategic focus? How subtle and sophisticated are your skills of influencing people more senior than you in the organisation? Do you stimulate debate and influence opinion?

How do you rate your personal characteristics against the following list:

I have a strong personal sense of purpose	Yes/No
I am a truthful person	Yes/No

I have respect for the views of others and expect them to have respect for mine	Yes/No
I have a lightness of touch and humility when dealing with more assertive managers, which I believe generates respect for me and enables me to influence their decision making	Yes/No
I love to explore new ideas and keep abreast of current developments	Yes/No
I am happy to stimulate debate, based on my own convictions, ready to challenge prevailing wisdom where necessary	Yes/No
I am normally confident in my own abilities	Yes/No
I believe that public agencies should have an HR function, or access to an outsourced or shared services function	Yes/No
I am keen to lead *a next generation HR function*.	Yes/No

None of these questions is asked in a judgemental way, since no one except you needs to know the answers you have given to them. However, again your answers should enable you to assess any areas which your personal development plan should seek to respond to: to make you an even better HR practitioner.

Concluding remarks

This essay has brought the book full circle from some of the challenges in Essay 1 and the examination of models of HR in Essay 2, to the way in which the reader as an individual might react to the output of some of the most up-to-date research into the HR function globally. The essay was intended to stimulate thought and debate about the direction the function is moving in the public sector, especially against some of the more pessimistic views cited in Essay 9 in particular. It is hoped that it satisfactorily concludes what the Preface admitted was a very brief overview of a massive area of management. After all, since most organisations claim that the people who work for them are their *most valued assets*, it is critical to give time to review how they are managed and how that management might be even more cost effective and value-added.

No one can deny the pressures that the public sector is under in most countries of the world. It is incumbent on the practitioners in the HR function to demonstrate individually and collectively that they have an important contribution to make to ensure that the sector is able to deliver the services that citizens require to the fullest extent possible, through the generation of innovative and insightful solutions.

References

Beer, Michael, Spector, Bert, Lawrence, Paul R, Qinn Mills, D and Walton, Richard E (1984) *Managing Human Assets: The Groundbreaking Harvard Business School Program.* The Free Press, New York

Brockett, James (2010) 'See HR as a professional services firm, says Ulrich', *People Management*, 25 March 2010, p11

Buyens, D and de Vos, A (1999) writing in *International HRM: Contemporary Issues in Europe*, eds Brewster C and Harris, H, Routledge, London

Calo, Thomas J (2010) 'Workforce and succession planning: no longer a zero-sum game', *HR News* (IPMA-HR), September 2010, pp.9–11

Chartered Institute of Personnel and Development (2010) *The truth about HR: the inside track on careers in human resources*, CIPD, London, at http://www.cipd.co.uk/NR/rdonlyres/D394EEAB-B886-4400-90AA-A539F226B12A/0/The_truth_about_HR.pdf

Chartered Institute of Personnel and Development (2010) *HRM Profession Map*, at www.cipd.co.uk/hr-profession-map

Chartered Institute of Personnel and Development (2010) *Shaping the future: sustaining organisational performance*, at http://www.cipd.co.uk/shapingthefuture?vanity=http://www.cipd.co.uk/stf

Chartered Institute of Personnel and Development (2010) *Sustainable organisation performance: what really makes the difference?* CIPD, London, at http://www.cipd.co.uk/NR/rdonlyres/69BF5AEA-7240-4F51-A437-BC165AA9B03E/0/Sustainable_organisation_performance_STF_interim_report.pdf

Chartered Institute of Personnel and Development (2010) *Time for change – towards a next generation of HR*, CIPD, London, at http://www.cipd.co.uk/NR/rdonlyres/062572E2-917A-48D5-861A-C44EFC8805CC/0/5126Nextgenthoughtpiece.pdf

Holbeche, Linda (2009) *Aligning Human Resources and Business Strategy*, 2nd ed, Butterworth-Heinemann, Oxford

Truss, Catherine (2009) 'Changing HR functional forms in the UK public sector', *The International Journal of Human Resource Management*, 20: 4, 717–737

Ulrich, Dave, Allen, Justin, Brockbank, Wayne, Younger, Jon and Nyman, Mark (2009) *HR Transformation: Building human resources from the outside in*, McGraw Hill, New York

Ulrich, Dave and Beatty, Dick (2001) 'From partners to players: extending the HR playing field', *Human Resource Management*, Winter 2001, Vol 40, No 4, pp.293–307, © 2001 John Wiley and Sons, Inc

Ulrich, D and Lake, D (1990) *Organizational capability: Competing from the inside out*, Wiley, New York

Wain, Daniel (2010) 'Add value, not spin', *People Management*, 20 May 2010

Postscript

In my Preface, I wrote that the world of the public sector was changing rapidly, even as we completed the draft of the book at the end of October 2010. In the three months between then and proof reading the final text at the end of January 2011, there were yet more signs of the changing dynamic in which the public sector is operating.

Here, by way of evidence, are just a few items from recent media reports:

economic issues:
- in the UK, Manchester City Council announced that it will need to reduce its labour force by about 2000 employees. Almost every other public agency in the UK is planning to cut their labour force during the coming years;
- in Portugal, the pay of public servants has been unilaterally cut from January 2011, adding to the number of countries in which public sector employees are subject either to a wage freeze or to enforced pay cuts;
- in the USA, there is some easing on staffing in many public sector agencies, but others continue to impose cuts in the labour force, or in pay and conditions.

demographic issues
- in the UK, it is now estimated that 10% (or 6 million) of the current population can expect to reach the age of 100. This is more than six times the current number of people in the population who are over 100. This suggests a need for service and labour market planning now to meet the needs arising over the next 50 years.

political issues
- the people of Ireland will have had a general election by the

time you read this book, following the collapse of its previous government as a result of the way it has handled the economic crisis.

organisational issues
- there is an increasing trend towards the introduction of shared services. In the UK two neighbouring local authorities recently advertised jointly for a chief executive who would advise and serve both of them;
- senior management costs continue to be reduced by combining services and functions into *super-departments*;

I think it is fair to say that, in all my 30 years' employment in HR in the public sector, and my 15 years in the academic sector, I rarely experienced the kind of continuing onslaught on public expenditure or the changes of operating environment that my successors are having to respond to today. Throughout the book, I have without apology stressed the need for a new kind of HR practitioner at the most senior level in the public sector, who is politically savvy and strategically focused, who knows and understands the business he or she is working in, and who can articulate that business into HR terms.

The task he or she faces may be lonely at times. It will certainly be challenging. It may be stressful and tiring. The reward, if the job is done successfully, will be in helping to sustain the delivery of quality key public services to its customers on a cost effective basis.

Dr Peter Smart
Aberdeen, Scotland

January 2011

Author index

Allen, David G 98, 102, 167
Allen, Justin 98, 153
Anthony, William P ... 117, 123, 125, 131, 137
Armstrong, Michael...35, 50, 103, 121, 125, 130, 137
Atkinson, John 77, 78, 79, 86, 88
Barber, I 103
Beatty, Dick 142, 144, 145, 153, 155, 167
Beer, Michael...19, 31, 33, 35, 36, 50, 134, 137, 141, 152, 162, 166
Bevan, S 98, 103
Bird, Hedda 109, 110, 113
Brewster, Chris...33, 40, 41, 42, 43, 50, 51, 152, 166
Broadfield, Ayson 89
Brockbank, Wayne 153, 167
Brockett, James 146, 147, 152, 160, 166
Buchanan, D A 81, 82, 88
Buyens, Dirk...33, 40, 41, 42, 43, 51, 56, 141, 152, 155, 161, 162, 163, 166
Calo, Thomas J 141, 152, 154, 166
Capelli, P 97, 103
Cheung-Judge, Mee-Yan 85, 89
Churchard, Claire 107, 108, 109, 113
Clarke, N 135, 138
Cooke, Mike 121, 125
de Vos, Ans...33, 40, 41, 42, 43, 51, 56, 141, 152, 155, 161, 162, 163, 166
East, Sam 110, 113
Edwards, Tony 35, 36, 51
Fincham, Robin 72, 77, 89
Fox, James C 116, 119, 125, 126
Fujishima, Noboru 107, 114
Gaebler, Ted 16, 31, 88, 89, 107, 114
Gennard, John 129, 137
Guest, David 33, 38, 39, 40, 51
Hammer, Michael 30, 80, 89
Handy, Charles B 77, 79, 86, 88, 89
Harrison, Rosemary 110, 114
Holbeche, Linda...33, 34, 51, 55, 58, 69, 85, 89, 141, 152, 162, 167
Judge, Graham 85, 89, 129, 137
Kacmar, K Michele 125, 137

Kelly, Geoff 116, 126, 131, 138
Kennerley, Liz 121, 126
Kimura, Seiki 92, 104, 112, 114
Knight, K 75, 89
Lake, D 144, 153, 155, 167
Lawrence, Paul R 31, 50, 137, 152, 166
MacLachlan, Rob 70, 149, 152
MacLeod, D 135, 138
McCalman, James 81, 82, 83, 88, 89
Nyman, Mark 153, 167
Osborne, David 16, 31, 88, 89, 107, 114
Paton, Robert A 81, 82, 83, 89
Perrewé, Pamela L 125, 137
Philpott, John 108
Pickard, Jane 31, 150, 153
Plastrik, Peter 88, 89
Popovich, Mark G 123, 126
Qinn Mills, D 31, 50, 137, 152, 166
Rashid, Noorzaman 123, 126
Rhodes, Peter S 72, 77, 89
Robinson, D 103
Rollison, Derek 72, 89
Shields, John 117, 121, 122, 123, 127
Shoesmith, Dean 108, 150
Sims, R R 134, 138
Smart, Peter ... 17, 72, 75, 76, 92, 104, 112, 114
Smedley, Tim 54, 56, 63, 69, 87, 90, 149, 153
Spector, Bert 31, 50, 137, 152, 166
Stevens, Michelle 150, 153
Truss, Catherine ... 145, 147, 151, 153, 154, 167
Ulrich, Dave...55, 56, 70, 142, 144, 145, 146, 147, 149, 152, 153, 155, 160, 162, 166, 167
van Ruyssevelde, Joris 47, 49, 51, 52
Wain, Daniel 142, 153, 154, 168
Walton, Richard E 31, 50, 137, 152, 166
Ward, Karen 95, 96, 105
Younger, Jon 153, 167

Subject index

Ageing population 25
Alzheimer's
- Alzheimer's Research Trust 26, 30
- dementia 26, 30
Asia(n) 47
Assessment centre(s) 96
Assessment tools
- Self-assessment tools 160
Australia 16, 27, 88, 127
Baby boomers 99
Belgium 40
Benchmarking 38, 68, 104
Best value 19, 151
Boston Consulting Group (BCG)
...12, 93, 94, 95, 96, 97, 99, 103, 129, 136, 137, 142, 152
Botswana 26, 28
Brazil 27
Budget(s)
- Budget cuts 8, 23, 99, 113, 135
- Budget deficits 23
Business process re-engineering 80, 86
Change management
- Model of perpetual transition management 82
- The 'seven C's of change' 84
Chartered Institute of Personnel and Development (CIPD)...12, 33, 44, 45, 46, 47, 51, 53, 56, 58, 62, 64, 65, 66, 67, 68, 69, 81, 84, 87, 88, 89, 93, 98, 103, 108, 113, 114, 124, 125, 126, 132, 133, 135, 136, 137, 138, 140, 141, 147, 149, 150, 152, 154, 155, 156, 157, 158, 159, 161, 162, 163, 166, 167
China/Chinese...21, 25, 34, 44, 47, 48, 49, 50, 52
Competency/competencies
...18, 22, 25, 29, 53, 54, 59, 61, 69, 72, 73, 77, 94, 106, 108, 119, 121, 122, 123, 125
Competitive tendering...15, 16, 19, 86, 107, 151

Comprehensive spending review 8
Convention of Scottish Local Authorities ... 130
Culture and traditions 20, 112
Customers
- Customer expectations 59
Demography/demographic
.... 10, 14, 15, 25, 26, 28, 30, 38, 99, 169
Denmark 20, 112
Deregulation 16
Downsizing 24, 77
Early retirement 9, 61, 86
Employee relations
- Employee commitment 40, 129, 134
- Employee engagement .. 66, 129, 134, 135, 136, 137, 138
- Employee involvement 130, 134
- Labour relations 42, 49
Employment legislation/law
........................22, 29, 60, 86, 128, 143, 148
Empowerment 73, 77, 136
Environment
- Environmental 28, 35
Equalities and diversity 99
Estonia 21
Financial constraints/financial pressures
....8, 53, 63
Finland 18
Flexible firm
- Atkinson's Model of the Flexible Firm 78
Flexible working 27, 77
France/French 8, 16, 73, 101, 135
Franchising 16, 21
Germany 18
Global recession
- Global economy 22
- Global economic crisis 14, 15, 24
Greece 8, 16, 23, 101, 135
Gross domestic product (GDP) 16
HIV/AIDS 26, 28
HR Bulletin 146, 152
HR News 141, 142, 152, 166

Subject index

Human resource management
- HR practitioner(s)/specialist(s)/professional(s) ...9, 11, 16, 22, 29, 30, 42, 43, 45, 54, 55, 56, 57, 59, 62, 63, 65, 86, 125, 140, 142, 145, 150, 155, 165, 170
- HR strategies 15, 26, 39, 54, 59

Immigration 27
Improvement Service (for Scottish Local Government) 19, 32, 68, 87, 99, 104, 111
Information and communications technology (ICT) ...9, 24, 25, 30, 58, 61, 73, 74, 77, 80, 109, 146, 148
International Public Management Association for Human Resources (IPMA-HR) ...32, 58, 68, 87, 95, 96, 99, 101, 104, 112, 124, 126, 146, 147, 152, 154, 166
Ireland 8, 135, 169
Italy 23, 27
Japan(ese)
- Japan Intercultural Academy of Municipalities 59, 69, 104, 112, 114

Job design
- Job enrichment 81
- Job enlargement 81
- Job rotation 81, 93

Kaizen 9, 80, 86, 148
Kennedy School of Government, Harvard University 32
Knowledge ... 10, 11, 18, 19, 25, 26, 29, 42, 44, 48, 54, 56, 60, 61, 72, 73, 77, 81, 106, 119, 121, 122, 133, 135, 146, 149

Kwansei Gakuin University
- Institute of Business and Accounting 11, 19, 32

Labour market ...18, 27, 28, 29, 30, 35, 60, 61, 63, 77, 93, 95, 99, 100, 163, 169

Leadership
- Leadership skills 22, 108, 109, 149

Learning ...55, 56, 65, 66, 71, 76, 84, 93, 106, 107, 109, 110, 111, 113, 114, 117, 123

Life expectancy 25, 26, 28, 31
Local Government Employers 92, 120, 124, 126, 130

Matrix organisations
- Matrix management 75, 89

Models of human resource management
- Added value/Value added model of HRM 40, 41, 42
- Buyens and de Vos model 40
- CIPD HR Profession Map 44, 56, 161, 162, 163
- European models 38, 43, 44, 50
- Guest's model of HRM 38, 39
- Harvard model 37, 38, 44

National Health Service (NHS) 8, 20, 23, 27, 68, 131, 150, 153, 156
Netherlands, The 30, 99
New models of service delivery 9
New public management 16, 30, 37, 86, 88, 107
New Zealand 16, 88, 107
Next generation HR ...147, 155, 156, 158, 159, 164, 165
Office of Manpower Economics 131, 138
Organisational citizenship 123, 134
Organisation design and development
- Organisational structure ...9, 13, 22, 63, 72, 75, 77, 80, 85, 86, 107, 108
- Organisational relationships 74, 75
- Principles of organisation design 71, 72, 86

Outsourcing
- Outsourcing services 74

Pay
- Pay freeze 8
- Pay review bodies 131
- Pay structures 9, 124, 125

People Management (journal of the CIPD) ...14, 15, 16, 31, 55, 57, 69, 70, 90, 113, 114, 140, 142, 152, 153, 166, 168

Political
- approach 14
- decision making/decision makers 10, 17, 38, 107
- thinking 18, 71

Portugal 23, 169
Privatisation 16, 21

Subject index

Project teams 75
Psychological contract.................. 130, 134, 138
Public Sector People Managers' Association
.... 32, 58, 69, 108
Public sector/public services
- activity 20
- cost efficient/cost efficiency 19, 24
- cost effectiveness.................... 38, 53, 73, 110
- delivery...9, 15, 16, 18, 22, 25, 29, 46, 55, 58, 59, 73, 74, 108, 111, 128, 129, 130, 136, 143, 144, 145, 146, 147, 151, 159, 170
Public Strategies Group 19
Recruitment...9, 26, 27, 39, 40, 48, 61, 65, 71, 91, 93, 94, 95, 100, 103, 104, 119, 144
Reinventing Government...16, 31, 86, 88, 107, 114
Resourcing.......... 14, 48, 66, 91, 92, 93, 100, 101
Retirement
- default retirement age........................27, 100
- pensions............................ 100, 124, 125, 132
Reward
- broad banding................ 119, 120, 124, 126
- high performance culture 115
- pay systems................................ 116, 124, 126
- performance and reward 37, 115, 124
- performance criteria............................22, 123
- performance management 22, 119, 121, 122, 123, 124, 125, 157
- performance related pay/rewards
.... 117, 121, 124, 136
- reward management 117
- reward systems 25, 36, 37, 39, 115, 117
- single status............. 119, 120, 126, 127 131
- total remuneration and total reward 117
Shamrock organisation 77, 79
Shared services
- HR business partner model 144
- partnering 24, 46
- shared services organisation(s) 146
Society for Human Resource Management (SHRM)... 54, 58, 70, 102, 104, 136, 138
Society of Local Authority Chief Executives (SOLACE) 95, 96, 104

South Africa... 26
Soviet
- former Soviet states.....................................21
- Soviet Union 21
Spain 8, 16, 23, 27, 101, 135
Strategy
- HR strategy 46, 55, 62, 68, 69, 157, 162, 163
- Strategic insights 37, 46, 54, 55, 57, 59, 60
Structure of the public sector
- Organisational structure(s)
...9, 13, 22, 63, 72, 75, 77, 80, 85, 86, 107, 108
- Management relationships 9
- Staffing structures 15
Sub-Saharan Africa 26, 28
Succession planning ... 71, 91, 94, 99, 100, 103, 152, 166
Sunday Times, The 95
Sweden
- Swedish Association for Local and Regional Authorities (SALAR) 124, 127
Talent
- Talent development
...66, 93, 106, 107, 109, 110, 111, 112, 113, 157
- Talent management
...66, 91, 93, 94, 95, 96, 97, 101, 102, 103, 104, 105, 159
- Talent planning..... 48, 91, 92, 93, 101, 106
- High potential employees .. 53, 94, 95, 107
Technology
- Technological developments....................24
Total Place 19, 31
Total quality management (TQM)
.... 9, 80, 86, 148
Training and development
- Retraining/reskilling 24, 61
UNISON 120, 127
United Kingdom (UK)
- England/English...8, 20, 21, 68, 73, 111, 130, 131
- Scotland..20, 68, 111
- Wales.............................21, 68, 111, 130, 131

- UK coalition government 23
United Nations
  - United Nations Department of Economic and Social Affairs (UNDESA)
    .... 28, 30, 31, 52
United States of America (USA)
  - US former Vice President Al Gore
    ....54, 87, 149
  - US government...23
Virtual organisation(s) 80
Workforce planning...60, 62, 63, 64, 65, 66, 67, 68, 94, 100, 119

Human resource management in the public sector

2011年3月31日　発行

著　者　Peter Smart, 稲澤克祐
発行者　宮原浩二郎
発行所　関西学院大学出版会
所在地　〒622-0891 兵庫県西宮市上ケ原一番町1-155
電　話　0798-53-7002

印　刷　協和印刷株式会社

©2011 by Peter Smart, Katsuhiro Inazawa
Printed in Japan by Kwansei Gakuin University Press
ISBN 978-4-86283-091-3
乱丁・落丁本はお取り替えいたします。
本書の全部または一部を無断で複写・複製することを禁じます。
http://www.kwansei.ac.jp/press